60.21

D1242144

AGING

THE
newbiology

AGING

Theories and Potential Therapies

Joseph Panno, Ph.D.

☑®
Facts On File, Inc.

AGING: Theories and Potential Therapies

Facts On File, Inc.
132 West 31st Street
New York NY 10001

MAY 11 2006

Library of Congress Cataloging-in-Publication Data
Panno, Joseph.
    Aging: theories and potential therapies / Joseph Panno.
        p. cm. — (The new biology)
    Includes bibliographical references and index.
    ISBN 0-8160-4951-3
    1. Aging. 2. Longevity. I. Title.
QP86.P33 2004
612.6'7—dc22   2003025469

Facts On File books are available at special discounts when purchased in bulk quantities for businesses, associations, institutions, or sales promotions. Please call our Special Sales Department in New York at (212) 967-8800 or (800) 322-8755.

You can find Facts On File on the World Wide Web at http://www.factsonfile.com

Text design by Erika K. Arroyo
Cover design by Pehrsson Design
Illustrations by Richard Garratt and Joseph Panno

Printed in the United States of America

MP FOF 10 9 8 7 6 5 4 3 2

This book is printed on acid-free paper.

For my wife, Diana,
who worked with me in the lab for many years,
and for my daughter Eleanor,
who knew about cells before she could read or write.

⊃✕⊂

CONTENTS

꘎

PREFACE

The New Biology set consists of the following six volumes: *The Cell, Animal Cloning, Stem Cell Research, Gene Therapy, Cancer,* and *Aging.* The set is intended primarily for middle and high school students, but it is also appropriate for first-year university students and the general public. In writing this set, I have tried to balance the need for a comprehensive presentation of the material, covering many complex fields, against the danger of burying—and thereby losing—young students under a mountain of detail. Thus the use of lengthy discussions and professional jargon has been kept to a minimum, and every attempt has been made to ensure that this be done without sacrificing the important elements of each topic. A large number of drawings are provided throughout the series to illustrate the subject matter.

The term *new biology* was coined in the 1970s with the introduction of recombinant DNA technology (or biotechnology). At that time, biology was largely a descriptive science in danger of going adrift. Microbiologists at the turn of the century had found cures for a few diseases, and biologists in the 1960s had cracked the genetic code, but there was still no way to study the function of a gene or the cell as a whole. Biotechnology changed all that, and scientists of the period referred to it as the new technique or the new biology. However, since that time it has become clear that the advent of biotechnology was only the first step toward a new biology, a biology that now includes nuclear transfer technology (animal cloning), gene therapy, and stem cell therapy. All these technologies are covered in the six volumes of this set.

The cell is at the very heart of the new biology and thus figures prominently in this book series. Biotechnology was specifically designed for studying cells, and using those techniques, scientists gained insights into cell structure and function that came with unprecedented detail.

As knowledge of the cell grew, the second wave of technologies—animal cloning, stem cell therapy, and gene therapy—began to appear throughout the 1980s and 1990s. The technologies and therapies of the new biology are now being used to treat a wide variety of medical disorders, and someday they may be used to repair a damaged heart, a severed spinal cord, and perhaps even reverse the aging process. These procedures are also being used to enhance food crops and the physical characteristics of dairy cows and to create genetically modified sheep that produce important pharmaceuticals. The last application alone could save millions of lives every year.

While the technologies of the new biology have produced some wonderful results, some of the procedures are very controversial. The ability to clone an animal or genetically engineer a plant raises a host of ethical questions and environmental concerns. Is a cloned animal a freak that we are creating for our entertainment, or is there a valid medical reason for producing such animals? Should we clone ourselves, or use the technology to re-create a loved one? Is the use of human embryonic stem cells to save a patient dying from leukemia a form of high-tech cannibalism? These and many other questions are discussed throughout the series.

The New Biology set is laid out in a specific order, indicated previously, that reflects the natural progression of the discipline. That is, knowledge of the cell came first, followed by animal cloning, stem cell therapy, and gene therapy. These technologies were then used to expand our knowledge of, and develop therapies for, cancer and aging. Although it is recommended that *The Cell* be read first, this is not essential. Volumes 2 through 6 contain extensive background material, located in the final chapter, on the cell and other new biology topics. Consequently, the reader may read the set in the order he or she prefers.

ACKNOWLEDGMENTS

I would first like to thank my friend and mentor, the late Dr. Karun Nair, for helping me understand some of the intricacies of the biological world and for encouraging me to seek that knowledge by looking beyond the narrow confines of any one discipline. The clarity and accuracy of the initial manuscript for this book was greatly improved by reviews and comments from Diana Dowsley and Michael Panno, and later by Frank Darmstadt, Executive Editor; Dorothy Cummings, Project Editor; and Anthony Sacramone, Copy Editor. I am also indebted to Ray Spangenburg, Kit Moser, Sharon O'Brien, and Diana Dowsley for their help in locating photographs for the New Biology set. Finally, I would like to thank my wife and daughter, to whom this book is dedicated, for the support and encouragement that all writers need and are eternally grateful for.

INTRODUCTION

✵

Everybody keeps getting older. It has been this way since multicellular creatures crawled out of the oceans more than 500 million years ago. Indeed, mortality and multicellularity seem to go hand in hand, for our unicellular ancestors, the protozoans and bacteria, have an indefinite life span. If we think of those ancestors as being a single lineage, it is a life form that has been alive for 3 billion years. There are those who think a human life span of 85 years is long enough, but compared with 3 billion years, it truly is the short end of the stick. There are, to be sure, many animals that have a shorter life span than we do: A horse has 20 years, a dog is lucky to see 15 summers, and the poor housefly is born and dead of old age in 30 days. On the other hand, a Galápagos tortoise and a sturgeon can live for 200 years.

On a cosmic scale, however, the difference in life span between a housefly and a sturgeon is puny, and besides, the comparison begs the question of why we age in the first place. After all, we have a reasonably good immune system; we heal well after being hurt; we have a group of enzymes that monitor and repair our DNA; and, as long as we eat well, our cells have plenty of energy to take care of themselves from day to day. Yet, despite all that, we get old with monotonous regularity. There appears to be neither rhyme nor reason to it. Some scientists think aging is due to evolutionary neglect: that natural selection was so busy finding ways to make us successful in the short term that it forgot to cover us in our old age. It is almost as though Mother Nature is saying, "I will do what I can to get you up to your reproductive years, so you can have offspring, but after that you are on your own."

Being on our own has meant that our bodies begin to break down soon after our peak reproductive years have past. The elderly cannot run as far, think as fast, or fight off infectious diseases nearly as well as they did when they were young. Moreover, one's physical appearance changes dramatically with age: The hair turns gray, muscle mass declines, the ears get bigger, and the skin becomes thin and wrinkled. At a more subtle level, men and women approaching their 80s converge on a common physical appearance; men become more feminine and women become more masculine. In men, this trend becomes apparent as the shoulders get narrower, the hips broader, the beard thinner, and the voice develops a higher pitch. In women, the shoulders become broader, the voice huskier, and hair begins to grow on the chin and upper lip. Gerontologists (scientists who study gerontology, or the mechanisms involved in the aging process), in noting these changes, have pondered one of the most difficult questions pertaining to the aging process: Is aging caused by the degenerative changes in a single organ, which then acts like an aging-clock for the rest of the body, or are all organs breaking down simultaneously?

Answering this question has proved to be extremely difficult. Researchers have studied age-related changes in virtually all tissues, organs, and organ systems (e.g., the endocrine system, consisting of many hormone-producing glands) of the body. Some evidence suggests that the brain may be an aging-clock that determines the rate at which the whole body ages, but the results of many other studies suggests that the rate at which an animal ages may be the sum of age-related changes occurring simultaneously in all parts of the body.

Consequently, the attempts to understand the aging process, involving such a complex system, have generated a large number of theories but few practical therapies. The therapies that are available are designed to treat diseases that are associated with aging, such as cancer and arthritis, but do not reverse the aging process itself. The recent trend in gerontology, particularly since the completion of the human genome project, is to search for genes that have a demonstrable effect on life span, the so-called longevity genes. Many such genes have been identified, and although the manipulation of these genes does not stop the aging process, they are providing many valuable insights into the cellular mechanisms of aging that may lead to the development of truly effecting antiaging therapies.

This book, another in the New Biology set, describes the field of gerontology and the many theories that scientists have developed over the years to explain the age-related changes that occur in virtually all animals. The first four chapters discuss the range of animal life spans relative to the human life span, aging theories, diseases that are associated with the aging process, and aging therapies (antiaging medicine). Subsequent chapters discuss the history of gerontology, the ongoing effort to find longevity genes, and the field of geriatrics, which uses our growing knowledge of the aging process to improve the quality of life for the elderly. The final chapter provides background material on cell biology, recombinant DNA technology, and other topics that are relevant to gerontology.

.1.

THE QUEST FOR IMMORTALITY

Concerns about human mortality date back at least 20,000 years when Cro-Magnons, the first *Homo sapiens,* prepared one of their own for burial. Cro-Magnon funerals are taken as evidence by anthropologists that those people thought like us. They knew about death, and in their sorrow, they adorned the corpse with prized possessions, possibly thinking they would be of use in a spiritual afterlife. In grieving for their lost loved ones, Cro-Magnons were drawn to a quest for immortality, but one that dealt with the soul rather than the body.

Distant relatives of the Cro-Magnons, living 4,000 years ago in Egypt, carried on the same tradition but on a colossal scale. Egyptian pharaohs were buried with all their worldly possessions and even a little food to see them on their way. According to their mythology, the dead, if accepted, could pass to the spirit world of the sun god, Amun-Ra, and his sister, Amunet, where they would live for eternity. The practice of burying the dead with all their belongings disappeared down through the millennia, but many people still believe in the eternal life of chosen spirits.

With the rise of science, and the appearance of powerful medical therapies, the quest for immortality has shifted from the spiritual to the physical. Although the origins of the scientific method can be traced back to the time of the Cro-Magnons, it did not assume its present form until the 20th century. Indeed, historians have noted that 90 percent of all scientists who have ever lived are still alive today.

The accomplishments of Louis Pasteur and other microbiologists at the turn of the last century and the explosive growth in biological research since then have provided cures for many terrible diseases: diphtheria, polio, and smallpox, to name but a few. These triumphs have given us reason to hope that someday we will be able to reverse the effects of age. If protozoans can live millions of years, why not the human body?

But so far, all attempts at physical rejuvenation have failed. Many such attempts date back to the turn of the early 1900s and involved the use of concoctions, potions, and even radioactive cocktails, often with disastrous results. One such concoction, popular in the 1920s, was Tho-Radia, a skin cream containing thorium and radium, two radioisotopes discovered by the great French physicist Marie Curie. The radioactive material was supposed to have an antiaging effect on the skin, but their use was abandoned when Curie and other scientists working with radioisotopes began having serious medical problems. Madame Curie developed cataracts, kidney failure, and a fatal leukemia, all from over-exposure to radioactive materials.

More recently, a new wave of antiaging therapies have been developed, employing everything from a shift in lifestyle to specific hormone supplements. Antiaging creams are still with us, only now the active ingredient is retinoic acid (vitamin A) instead of radium. Whether any of these treatments will be successful is in doubt, but the failures so far are like the first tentative steps of a toddler. We are only beginning to understand the tremendous complexities of the cell and the way an organism changes with time. As our science matures, we may be able to reverse some effects of age, but whether this leads to physical immortality is a hotly debated topic at the present time.

One Hour upon the Stage

When William Shakespeare in his play *Richard III* compared the human life span to one hour on the stage, he was being very generous. If our life span were indeed 1/24 of the 3 billion years that microbes have been alive, we would live 125 million years. As it is, our life span, on a 24-hour time scale, is but a wink of an eye.

Life spans vary considerably within the animal kingdom. In general, tiny animals bearing many offspring have short life spans, while large animals bearing few offspring live much longer. The fruit fly, *Drosophila melanogaster,* is an example of a small animal with a short life span. *Drosophila* have a maximum life span of 40 days, but most of them are dead in two weeks. These animals are called holometabolous insects because the eggs hatch into wormlike larvae that feed for a time before pupating, during which time the larvae metamorphose into the adult form. The newly emerged males and females waste no time in producing the next generation. The females mate within 24 hours, and throughout their short lives produce tens of thousands of offspring. In a survival strategy such as this, all the biological adaptations have focused on preservation of the species at the expense of the individual. Flies have many predators, and adaptations that could lengthen their life span would be useless, since the flies would be eaten long before their biological time was up.

Scanning electron micrograph (SEM) of the fruit fly *Drosophila melanogaster.* This little insect is about 3 mm long, is commonly found around spoiled fruit, and is an example of a very short-lived animal. It is also much studied by gerontologists and geneticists around the world. Mutant flies, with defects in any of several thousand genes, are available, and the entire genome has been sequenced. *(David M. Phillips/Photo Researchers, Inc.)*

Elephants, on the other hand, are large animals with few predators that produce a single offspring every five years. Elephants are mammals and, like all mammals, spend a great deal of time rearing and caring for their young. In this case, adaptations to increase their life span make a lot of sense. With reduced pressure from predators, the young can afford a leisurely developmental period, during which time the adults teach them how best to deal with their environment. The longer the adults live, the more things they learn, and the more they can pass on to their offspring. Consequently, these animals have a relatively long life span of 75 to 100 years, similar to that of humans. In general, long-lived animals tend to be rather intelligent, but there are some exceptions, the most notable of which are the sturgeon and the Galápagos tortoise.

The sturgeon is an extremely ancient fish that has existed for more than 200,000 years, predating the rise of the dinosaurs during the Jurassic period. They live in the oceans, seas, and rivers of North America, Europe, and Asia, where they often grow to a length of 20 feet and weigh a ton or more. Sturgeon eggs, called caviar, are considered to be a great delicacy in many parts of the world. The sturgeon is possibly the longest-lived animal that we know of, sometimes reaching 300 years or more, and yet they are no more intelligent than any other fish. Moreover, sturgeons, like most fish, have thousands of offspring each year and spend no time taking care of them. The sturgeon's strategy for longevity is simply to keep growing. They have hit upon a rule of nature that states that happy cells are dividing cells. As long as a sturgeon keeps growing, its longevity is regulated by external forces, such as accidents

African elephants (*Loxodonta africana*) in the Amboseli National Park, Kenya. These large, intelligent animals have a maximum life span of about 100 years, very similar to that of humans. *(Martin Harvey/Photo Researchers, Inc.)*

Giant tortoise from the Galápagos Islands (Santa Cruz Island). These animals have very long life spans that may exceed 200 years. (*Jeffrey Greenburg/Photo Researchers, Inc.*)

and predators, not by cellular senescence. Being a poikilotherm (cold-blooded animal) reinforces the sturgeon's continuous-growth strategy because it minimizes the growth rate and activity level of the animal. Continuous growth is a strategy that also explains the longevity of certain plants, such as the California redwood or the oak tree, which can live a thousand years or more.

Galápagos tortoises live on a group of islands off the coast of South America. They are large animals, sometimes weighing more than 500 pounds that can live for 200 to 250 years and usually give birth to a dozen offspring every year. They are not highly intelligent animals, at least not as mammals understand intelligence; nor do they spend any time taking care of their young. In fact, a tortoise never sees its young. The female lays the eggs in the sand, covers them over, and the rest is left to Mother Nature and a bit of luck. When the young hatch, they dig their way to the surface, a feat that takes a month to accomplish, and

A sculpture of an elderly couple in their 80s showing the general effects of age and the age-related convergence of physical characteristics described in the introduction. *(Dr. Joseph Panno)*

make straight for the water, which is usually 10 to 20 yards away. The dash for the water is made through a predator gauntlet, and many of the young tortoises are caught by seagulls along the way. Those that make it to the water are preyed upon by fish in the sea, and the few that survive to adulthood return to the beaches of their birth, where they live out the rest of their lives. The tortoise, unlike the sturgeon, reaches a standard adult size, so most of the cells in the adult's body become postmitotic, as occurs in mammals. The unusual longevity of this animal is believed to be due to its very low growth rate and, as it is a poikilotherm like the sturgeon, its low metabolic rate and activity level.

Humans have a maximum life span of more than 100 years. The longest-lived human on record was Jeanne Calment, a woman from Arles, France, who died in 1997 at the age of 122. As impressive as this is, it is a short life span indeed when compared with the record holder from the plant kingdom. This goes to Methuselah, a 4,600-year-old pine that lives on a mountainside in Arizona.

Growing Younger

Many gerontologists have claimed that it is impossible for individual humans to grow younger, because it would be too difficult to rejuvenate all the cells and organs of the body. Such claims need to be taken with a large grain of salt; it should be remembered that just five years before the first sheep was cloned, most scientists thought that cloning a mammal was biologically impossible. In addition, what we have learned about animal cloning and stem cells since 1996 suggests it may indeed be possible to produce a therapy that will allow an individual to grow younger.

Growing younger, at the cellular level, is analogous to the dedifferentiation of a cloned cell nucleus: Both are a matter of converting a cell from an aged phenotype (the physical expression of an organism's genes) to a youthful phenotype. In a sense, the cloning of a cell nucleus is the most successful attempt at rejuvenation that has yet been accomplished. In a cloning experiment, the cytoplasm of the recipient oocyte converts the donor nucleus from an aged phenotype to one that is capable of supporting full embryonic development. At the organismic level, this is equivalent to converting an adult to an embryo. If it can be done in one cell, it could be done in many. And if all the nuclei in an old person's body could be reprogrammed to a youthful phenotype, it would lead to the complete rejuvenation of all the cells in the body. If that happened, the individual would grow younger.

The Road Ahead

In 1900 life expectancy for the average North American was only 45 years. This has increased to the current expectancy of 80 years primarily because of a dramatic reduction in infant mortality, cures for various diseases, better hygiene, and better living conditions. This increase occurred despite the enormous number of deaths per year from cigarette smoking. A further increase of 20 to 30 years is expected if cures are found for cancer and cardiovascular disease. Beyond that, advances in life expectancy will have to wait for an improvement in our understanding of the basic mechanisms of cellular senescence.

Developing therapies that will reverse the aging process, allowing individuals to grow younger, is theoretically possible, but the realization of that goal will likely turn out to be the most difficult challenge that biologists have ever faced. The production of aging therapies will require a fusion of animal cloning, gene therapy, and stem cell technologies. But even these technologies, as powerful as they are, will not be enough. Gaining a deep understanding of the basic mechanisms of aging will require detailed information about every gene in our bodies and about what those genes are doing as we grow old. This information is only now being made available, but over the next few years, we should see real gains being made in the field of gerontology.

.2.
AGING THEORIES

Aging theories cover the genetic, biochemical, and physiological properties of a typical organism, and the way these properties change with time. Genetic theories deal with speculations regarding the identity of aging genes, accumulation of errors in the genetic machinery, programmed senescence, and telomeres. Biochemical theories are concerned with energy metabolism, generation of free radicals, the rate of living, and the health of mitochondria. Physiological theories deal almost entirely with the endocrine system and the role of hormones in regulating the rate of cellular senescence.

Error Catastrophe Theory

Running a cell is a complex affair. RNA and proteins have to be synthesized on a regular basis to maintain and run the cell's machinery (see chapter 8 for a cell primer). Production of proteins, either for enzymes or structural materials, occurs in a two-step process: transcription of the gene to produce mRNA, followed by translation of the message to produce the protein. For cells that are actively dividing, a third step, replication of the DNA, precedes the other two. Errors can occur all along the way; when they do, defective genes, mRNA, and proteins are produced. The error catastrophe theory, first proposed in the 1960s, suggests that over time, the number of errors build up to a catastrophic level leading to the death of the cell and, possibly, the entire organism.

Soon after this theory was proposed, many scientists conducted experiments that attempted to force a buildup of errors to see how the cells would cope with it. Bacteria were grown on a medium containing defective amino acids to maximize the error frequency of protein synthesis. Similar experiments were conducted on fruit flies (*Drosophila*) and mice, both of which were given food containing defective amino acids. To everyone's surprise, these experiments had no effect on the bacteria's or animal's health, vigor, or life span. Somehow the cells were able to avoid an error catastrophe. Today we understand why those experiments failed: Cells have elaborate repair systems and strategies that detect and destroy defective molecules. If a defective protein is synthesized, it is quickly broken down and replaced with a normal copy. Only in cases where the repair systems have been damaged would an error catastrophe occur (see Werner's syndrome in chapter 5).

In its original formulation, the error catastrophe theory focused on protein synthesis, which apparently can tolerate a high error frequency. Consequently, many scientists began to wonder if errors in the genome, or possibly a defective regulation of the genes, might be responsible for the aging process. After all, cells avoid an error catastrophe at the translational level because they can always try again with a fresh mRNA from a good gene. But if the genes themselves are damaged, or programmed for senescence, the outcome would be a gradual decline in cell vigor and the eventual death of the organism.

Genes and Programmed Aging

Are we programmed to get old? If we are, is it like the program that guides our development from a single fertilized egg to a multicellular organism? Or is aging the unfortunate side effect of adaptations that make it possible for us to have and protect our offspring? Many gerontologists believe that aging is a matter of evolutionary neglect, rather than design.

However life spans evolved, it is clear that our genes have the final say in how long we are going to be on the stage. Even though flies and humans are constructed from the same kinds of cells (eukaryotes), one animal lives two weeks, the other 80 years. If those eukaryotes had remained free-living, as their protozoan ancestors have done, they would live for millions of years.

The genes in a multicellular organism appear to be regulating life span for the good of the cell community as a whole. The size of the community, the animal's intelligence, the number of offspring, and the pressure the animal experiences from its predators, are all taken into account. The final life span seems to be a balance of all these forces and, given these forces, may be the best deal the organism can hope for. There would be no point to nature's producing a fruit fly that could live a thousand years, because their predators eat them all in a matter of days. Scientists might try producing a fly that could live that long, but what in the world would an animal with that level of intelligence do for all that time? This is not just a whimsical point. There is a very strong correlation between longevity and the weight of the brain: Smart animals live longer than dumb animals (with two exceptions, noted in chapter 1).

The goal of gerontologists is to try to get a better understanding of the covenant between the genes, the organism, and the environment. Whether intended by evolution or not, many genes are directly responsible for an animal's life span. These genes may be exerting their effects through inappropriate behavior (that is, they are turning on or off at the wrong time) or through a mutation that eventually damages the protein product.

Damage at the gene level re-invokes the error catastrophe theory, but many experiments have failed to establish a role for genetic (or somatic) mutations in cell senescence. This is because the cell can detect and repair DNA damage as easily as it deals with errors in translation, and those repair systems remain intact long after the animal shows visible signs of age.

The inappropriate expression of certain genes as a major cause of aging is only now being addressed in a comprehensive way. With the genome project now complete (see chapter 8), it will soon be possible to screen for the expression of all human genes, in every tissue and organ of the body. When this job is complete (and it will be as big a job as the genome project itself) we will finally have an idea of which genes are responsible for our life span.

Telomeres

Although we have not identified the genes controlling our life span, there is a genetic element called a telomere that clearly regulates the replicative life span of human cells in culture. A telomere is a simple DNA sequence that is repeated many times, located at the tips of each chromosome. Telomeres are not genes, but they are needed for the proper duplication of the chromosomes in dividing cells. Each time the chromosomes are duplicated, the telomeres shrink a bit, until they get so short the DNA replication machinery can no longer work. This occurs because the enzyme that duplicates the DNA (DNA polymerase) has to have some portion of the chromosome out ahead of it. Much like a train backing up on a track, DNA polymerase preserves a safe distance from the end of the DNA so it does not slip off the end. Telomeres also provide a guarantee that genes close to the ends of the chromosomes have been replicated. DNA polymerase stalls automatically whenever it gets too close to the end of the chromosome, permanently blocking the ability of the cell to divide. When this happens, the cell is said to have reached replicative senescence.

The telomeres in human fibroblasts are long enough to permit about 50 rounds of DNA replication. That is, the cell can divide about 50 times in culture. This is often referred to as the Hayflick limit, after Leonard Hayflick, the scientist who was the first to notice that normal cells cannot divide indefinitely in culture. Cancer cells, on the other hand, can divide indefinitely, and from them scientists isolated an enzyme called telomerase that restores the telomeres after each cell division. If the telomerase gene is added to normal fibroblasts, they are no longer bound by the Hayflick limit and can divide indefinitely, like an immortal cancer cell. The transformation of normal fibroblasts with the telomerase gene was conducted for the first time in 1998 at the Geron Corporation, a biotechnology company. The results generated a tremendous amount of excitement, for they seemed to imply that reversal of replicative senescence would be followed very quickly by the reversal of the aging process. Scientists at Geron began talking about human life spans of several hundred years.

Experiments since have shown, however, that while telomerase can block replicative senescence in cultured cells, it has little to do with the life span of the animal as a whole. Indeed some animals with long life spans have short telomeres and negligible telomerase activity, while other animals with short life spans have long telomeres and active telomerase. This is not surprising if we keep in mind that most cells in an animal's body are postmitotic; they stop dividing soon after the individual is born. So the life span of the individual made from those cells cannot be regulated by the length of the telomeres.

Rate-of-Living Theory

This theory takes a pragmatic approach to the regulation of life span. Simply put, it claims that if you are going to live fast and hard, your life will be short. The engine in a race car, run at full throttle, is lucky to last a full day. On the other hand, engines that are driven carefully, at modest RPMs, can last for 10 to 20 years and may even log 200,000 miles. Of course, if you buy a new car, park it in a garage, and rarely drive it, it will last even longer. This theory is not concerned with the underlying mechanism of aging, but simply advocates repair or replacement of body parts as they wear out, much in the way we deal with a broken-down car.

Of course, some body parts, such as our brain and muscles, cannot be replaced, and if anything serious happens to them, it would likely be fatal. The rate-of-living theory tries to deal with this fatal scenario by adopting a preventive strategy, involving a reduction in activity level and caloric intake. These strategies have been tested in houseflies, mice, and rats with some success.

Houseflies normally live one month in laboratory conditions, that is, in a large cage where they are fed and protected from their predators. If they are kept in tiny cages, no bigger than a teacup, their flight activity is severely restricted, and as a consequence, their life span is more than doubled. Caloric restriction has the same effect, but is most likely due to the forced reduction in flight activity, due to a lack of energy. Raising mice or rats in confined quarters to lower their activity level has no effect and may even reduce the life span because of the stress it causes in these animals. Caloric restriction, however, can increase a rat's life span by 50 to 60 percent. While impressive, this is not a therapy that is recommended for humans. *Caloric restriction* is really another way of saying *starvation diet,* and no one would opt for a therapy that involves eating so little food that the individual barely has strength to get out of bed in the morning. However, a moderate limitation on caloric intake could still add 10 to 20 years to one's life span.

Free Radicals

The role of free radicals is closely related to the rate-of-living theory and was originally proposed in the 1950s. Free radicals are molecules that have an unpaired electron, which makes them very reactive. One of the most important, the oxygen free radical, is a toxic exhaust produced by mitochondria during the very important metabolic process of oxidative phosphorylation. This process produces the ATP that cells need to survive. The oxygen free radical can remove an electron from virtually any molecule in the cell, including DNA, RNA, proteins, and the lipids in the cell membrane. When it does so, it triggers a chain reaction of destabilized molecules reacting with other molecules to form new free radicals and a variety of potentially dangerous compounds. Many gerontologists believe free radicals are directly responsible for cellular senescence and the aging of the animal as a whole.

However, cells do not allow free radicals free rein. A special enzyme, called superoxide dismutase (SOD), neutralizes oxygen free radicals as they are produced. Gerontologists in favor of the free radical theory maintain that SOD does not neutralize all the free radicals and that the damage is done by those that escape. Alternatively, aging may reduce the efficiency of SOD, such that the amount of free radicals increases gradually with age. An antiaging remedy, consisting of a regular diet of antioxidants (chemicals that deactivate free radicals) such as vitamin E or vitamin C, has been proposed. Many experiments have been conducted on mice and rats to test this remedy but with limited success.

Hormone Imbalance Theory

Coordination of an animal's physiology is the job of the endocrine system. This system consists of a command center located in a part of the brain called the hypothalamus; a master endocrine gland called the pituitary, which is connected directly to the hypothalamus; and a variety of secondary endocrine glands located in various parts of the body. The hypothalamus controls the pituitary by releasing hormone messengers that pass directly to the gland, where they stimulate or inhibit the release of pituitary hormones. The pituitary hormones, released into the blood, control the activity of other glands, such as the adrenal and

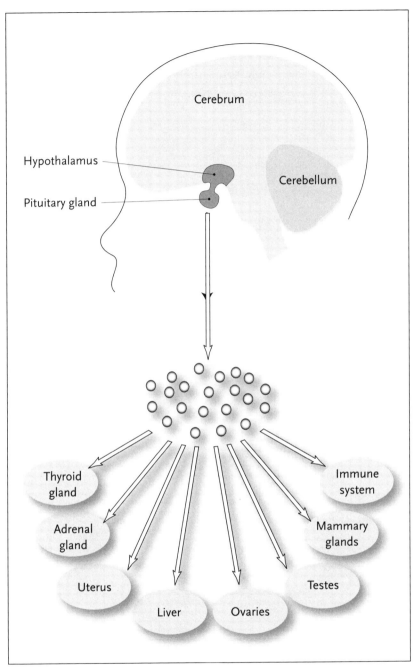

The human endocrine system is controlled by the hypothalamus, which regulates the production and release of various hormones from the pituitary gland. The pituitary hormones, in turn, regulate other glands, tissues, and organs of the body.

thyroid glands, as well as organs such as the ovaries, testes, and liver. All the hypothalamic messengers and the pituitary hormones are small proteins. Overall, the system is responsible for regulating reproductive

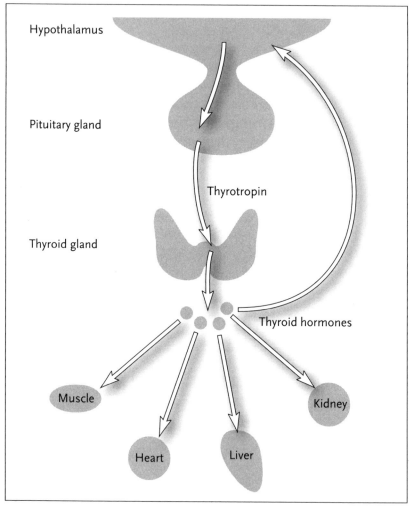

Regulation of the endocrine system. The hypothalamus instructs the pituitary gland to release thyroid-stimulating hormone (TSH), leading to secretion of thyroid hormones, which stimulate the activity of several organs. Thyroid hormone levels are monitored by the hypothalamus. When they get too high, TSH release is reduced or stopped.

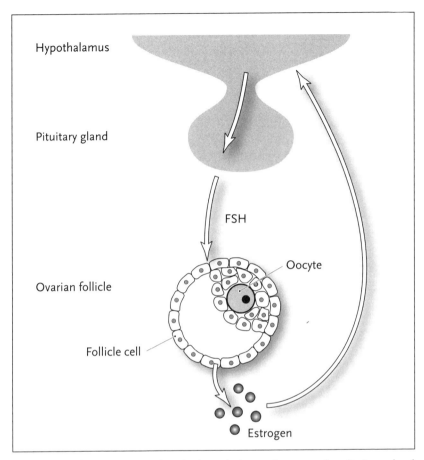

Hypothalamus

Pituitary gland

FSH

Ovarian follicle

Oocyte

Follicle cell

Estrogen

Regulation of the ovarian cycle. The hypothalamus instructs the pituitary gland to release follicle-stimulating hormone (FSH), promoting maturation of ovarian follicle cells, which in turn begin synthesizing and releasing estrogen. Low estrogen levels stimulate FSH release. High levels of estrogen inhibit the release of FSH but stimulate the release of a pituitary hormone (not shown) that initiates ovulation.

cycles, growth, energy metabolism, storage and mobilization of food molecules, and the fight-or-flight response (see table on pages 18–19).

The endocrine system is self-regulating, as illustrated by the control of the thyroid gland. The hypothalamus releases a messenger molecule called thyrotropin-releasing hormone, which stimulates the release of

HORMONES OF THE PITUITARY GLAND	
Hormone	**Description**
Adrenocorticotropin (ACTH)	This hormone stimulates release of adrenaline and other steroids from the adrenal cortex. Adrenaline is involved in the "flight or fight" response. ACTH is controlled by a hypothalamic messenger called corticotropin-releasing hormone.
Antidiuretic hormone (ADH)	ADH promotes water conservation by the kidneys. It is controlled by sensors that monitor the degree of body dehydration.
Follicle-stimulating hormone (FSH)	This hormone promotes development of sperm in the male and oocyte follicles in the female. Its release is controlled by a hypothalamic messenger called FSH-releasing hormone.
Growth hormone (GH)	GH stimulates the uptake of glucose and amino acids by all tissues (except neurons). Its release is blocked by a hypothalamic messenger called GH-inhibiting hormone.

thyrotropin (also known as thyroid-stimulating hormone) from the pituitary. Thyrotropin, in turn, stimulates the thyroid gland to release thyroid hormones, the most important of which is thyroxine, a hormone that stimulates cell metabolism and growth. The self-regulating feature of this system is the ability of the hypothalamus to monitor the level of thyroxine in the blood. When it gets too high, the hypothalamus signals the pituitary to cut back on the release of thyrotropin, or to stop releasing it altogether.

The regulation of the human female reproductive, or ovarian, cycle involves the same general scheme. In this case, the hypothalamus releases a molecule called gonadotropin-releasing factor, which stimulates the pituitary to release follicle-stimulating hormone (FSH). FSH

Hormone	Description
Luteinizing hormone (LH)	LH stimulates synthesis of testosterone by the testes and ovulation in females. Its release is controlled by a hypothalamic messenger called LH-releasing hormone.
Oxytocin	Oxytocin stimulates uterine contractions during childbirth and the release of milk from mammary glands. Its release is stimulated by cervical distension and suckling.
Prolactin	Prolactin stimulates the growth of mammary glands and milk production. Its release is blocked by a hypothalamic messenger called prolactin-inhibiting hormone.
Thyrotropin	This hormone initiates the release of thyroid hormones from the thyroid gland. Thyroid hormones are growth factors that stimulate cellular activity and growth. The release of thyrotropin is controlled by a hypothalamic messenger called thyrotropin-releasing hormone (TRH).

stimulates growth and development of ovarian follicles, each of which contain an oocyte. As the follicle cells mature, they synthesize and release the female hormone estrogen into the blood. The hypothalamus monitors the level of estrogen in the blood. Low levels of estrogen result in continuous release of FSH from the pituitary gland, but high levels, achieved when the follicle is mature, cause the hypothalamus to block release of FSH from the pituitary and, at the same time, to stimulate release of luteinizing hormone (LH) to trigger ovulation. If the mature oocyte is fertilized and successfully implants in the uterus, cells surrounding the embryo produce large amounts of estrogen to prepare the mother's body for the pregnancy and to block further release of FSH. If the egg is not fertilized, estrogen levels drop, signaling the hypothalamus to stimulate renewed synthesis and release of FSH to complete the cycle. FSH also promotes development of sperm in the male (see the accompanying table).

Given its breadth of influence, it is no wonder the endocrine system has captured the attention of gerontologists, many of whom believe that aging of the organism as a whole begins with the senescence of the hypothalamus. In this sense, the hypothalamus is like a clock that regulates the rate at which the individual grows older. With the age-related failure of the command center, hormonal levels of the body begin to change, and this in turn produces the physical symptoms of age.

One of the most dramatic age-related changes in humans is the loss of the ovarian cycle in females, generally referred to as the onset of menopause. Menopause usually occurs as women reach 50 years of age and is marked by a cessation in the development of ovarian follicles and, as a consequence, a dramatic drop in estrogen levels. Estrogen, aside from its role in reproduction, is important to female physiology for the maintenance of secondary sexual characteristics, skin tone, and bone development. Female mice and rats also go through menopause, although in these animals it is called diestrous, or the cessation of the estrous cycle.

For gerontologists, the onset of menopause in mice and rats provides an experimental system which can be used to test the idea that the hypothalamus is an aging-clock; that is, menopause or diestrous occurs because the hypothalamus stops releasing the necessary messenger molecules. When this happens, the reproductive system grinds to a halt. Many experiments were conducted in which pituitary glands or ovaries from old female rats were transplanted into young rats. In general, they showed that old pituitary glands functioned well in young bodies, and that old ovaries regained their estrous cycle. When prepubertal ovaries were transplanted to old female rats, the majority of them fail to regain their cycles. Similarly, when young pituitaries are transplanted into old rats, they are usually unable to support a normal estrous cycle.

Additional evidence in support of the role of the hypothalamus in the aging process comes from the observation that the levels of pituitary hormones, with the exception of ACTH, gradually decrease with age. The overall effect of this change is believed to be the loss of vigor, physical strength, and endurance that is typical in an aging human.

Accordingly, many attempts have been made to reverse these effects with hormone therapies that include GH, estrogen, or testosterone supplements. While these therapies have alleviated some of the symptoms of old age, they have not been able to reverse the aging process. With our limited knowledge of the cell and the complexities of physiological and endocrinological systems, there are real dangers associated with hormone therapies. Estrogen supplements can minimize bone thinning in menopausal women, but constant exposure to this hormone can lead to breast cancer. Similarly, androgen supplements in men can increase vigor and physical strength, but constant exposure to testosterone, and estrogen, is known to be a leading cause of prostate cancer. Growth hormone supplements suffer from similar problems in that they can induce cancers; they can also lead to the development of bone deformations.

Despite its great promise and the fact that it has generated some useful geriatric therapies, the hormonal disregulation or imbalance theory has failed to produce a definitive model of the aging process; nor have any of the hormonal therapies inspired by this theory been able to reverse the effects of age. Instead, the application of this theory, as with the other theories already discussed, merely allows a somewhat healthier old age, an effect which can also be obtained simply by eating well and getting lots of fresh air and exercise.

Concluding Remarks

With the exception of the role of telomeres in aging, all the theories just described have been with us for more than 40 years, and during that time gerontologists have subjected those theories to thousands of experiments in the hope of gaining a better understanding of the aging process. But today we do not understand the underlying mechanism of aging any better than we did when those theories were first formulated. This is not a criticism of the many outstanding scientists who devoted their research lives to this problem, but a recognition of the tremendous complexities involved in the aging process. Aging is the puzzle of all centuries, and its resolution will take an effort that will dwarf all other biological research projects to date.

We simply do not know enough about the behavior of our genes as we grow old, but the recent completion of the human genome project is

Microarray analysis of gene expression. Fragments of genes are spotted onto a glass microscope slide to produce a two-dimensional array. Labeled mRNA is hybridized to the array to determine which genes are active (white spots) and which are not (gray spots). This simulated array shows the expression of 100 genes.

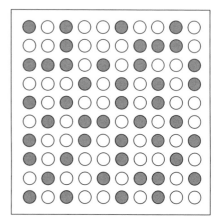

providing the information necessary for a fresh start. Scientists will soon be able to determine the behavior of all 30,000 human genes, in every organ and tissue of the body, throughout the human life span. The effort has already begun. Scientists at the University of Wisconsin have recently reported the results of a study in which they evaluated the activity of 20,000 genes in cells from the prostate gland, before and after the cells attained replicative senescence.

This type of study is made possible by the production of DNA microarrays. Based on information provided by the genome project, a short piece of every available gene is spotted onto a solid support (usually, a specially treated glass microscope slide), then hybridized with labeled mRNA isolated from chosen cells. If a gene is active in the cell, its mRNA will bind to the piece of that gene attached to the microarray, effectively labeling that particular point, or pixel, on the array. Computers are used to compare the young and old cells, spot by spot, to gain a final estimate of expression for every gene represented on the array.

Microarray analysis provides an extremely powerful method for analyzing the aging process in an unbiased manner. That is, until the genome project was completed, gerontologists, using available theories as a guide, had to make an educated guess as to which genes might be involved in cellular senescence. Studies were then designed around these genes in a few of the animal's tissues or organs. It is clear now that such a limited approach is doomed to failure. Aging is a highly integrated phenomenon, involving all the organs and tissues of the body.

Some tissues or organs may age at their own rates, but they are all part of the same process.

Evaluating all the human genes will be an enormous job that will take many years to complete. With more than 20 different organs and tissues in the human body, representing 200 cell types, such an undertaking will tax the resources of the science community. There are many obstacles to overcome, such as acquisition of the tissue, most of which will have to be obtained from deceased humans. Similar studies may also be conducted on flies, mice, and rats as their genomes are sequenced and microarrays become available. This is a big job, but one that will finally give us an understanding of how and why animals grow old.

·3·
AGE-RELATED DISEASES

Growing old holds many pleasures, but for someone with Alzheimer's disease (AD), it can be a confusing and often frightening experience. The image of an absentminded elderly man or woman has been with us for a long time. People today are in the habit of thinking that this is the natural consequence of growing old, but gerontologists (scientists who study the aging process) have taught us to be cautious of this stereotype. Old people may be slower at certain tasks, but they are not necessarily senile or any more absentminded than a 20-year-old. Aging makes us more susceptible to certain diseases, but those diseases are not an inevitable consequence of growing old. Several other age-related diseases are described in this chapter, but none are so devastating as AD.

Alzheimer's Disease

Alzheimer's disease is a neurological disorder affecting the central nervous system (CNS) that leads to a progressive loss of memory, language, and the ability to recognize friends and family. The average course of the disease, from early symptoms to complete loss of cognitive ability, is 10 years. Alois Alzheimer first described AD in 1907, and it has since become the fourth-leading cause of death among the elderly. The incidence of this disease increases with age and is twice as common in women as in men. In 2004 more than 4.5 million Americans were suffering from AD. Worldwide, there are several million recorded cases, but because poor medical facilities and diagnostic procedures in many parts of the world result in underreporting of the disease, the real number could be as high as 15 million cases.

The human CNS is divided into the cerebrum (the main portion of the brain, including the cerebral cortex), the cerebellum, and the brain stem. The cerebrum is the home of human intellect and the source of individual personality. It also processes and analyzes information from all the sensory nerves of the body. A special area of the cerebrum called the hippocampus is important for processing memories for long-term storage in other parts of the brain. The cerebellum regulates fine motor control over our muscles, making it possible for a person to learn how to play the piano, manipulate fine objects with precise control, and perform other activities that require intricate coordination. The brain stem is in control of our automatic functions, such as the rate at which the heart beats, the contraction of muscles of the digestive tract, and respiratory rate. It also controls our ability to sleep and to stay awake.

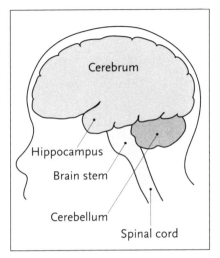

The human central nervous system. The human brain consists of the cerebrum, the cerebellum, and the brain stem, which is continuous with the spinal cord. The brain and spinal cord are called the central nervous system (CNS). The hippocampus, lying beneath the surface of the brain, coordinates memory functions.

AD begins in the hippocampus; during the early stages, known as preclinical AD, some damage occurs to the brain, but not enough to produce outward signs of the disease. Over a period of years, AD spreads to many areas of the cerebrum. Three genes have been identified that are associated with the onset of AD. The first of these is *tau*, which codes for a protein needed for the construction of microtubules. The second gene, *app* (codes for amyloid precursor protein, APP), codes for a protein that is embedded in the cell membrane. The third gene, *sen* (senilin, also known as presenilin), codes for an enzyme that

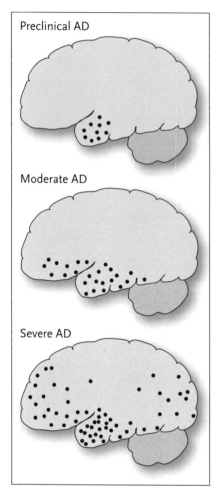

Preclinical AD

Moderate AD

Severe AD

Progression of AD. Alzheimer's disease (black circles) begins in the hippocampus, spreading over a period of years to affect several regions of the cerebrum.

may be involved in processing APP. Defects in any of these genes leads to the extensive death of neurons that is characteristic of AD.

Neurons are remarkable cells, specially designed for communication. A signal, in the form of an electrochemical jolt, enters a neuron at its dendrites and is passed along to another neuron through the axon, a process that takes less than a microsecond. Neural circuits are constructed when axons make contact with the dendrites of other neurons. The connection between an axon and a dendrite is called a synapse. Circuits in the human brain consist of billions of neurons, each forming thousands of synaptic junctions with other neurons. These circuits give us our intellect, emotions, vision, and the ability to recognize our friends and loved ones.

Although neurons communicate through the synapse, they do not actually touch one another. Close inspection of a synapse shows a small gap separating the axon from the dendrite. A signal is transmitted across the gap by the release of small proteins called neurotransmitters, which are stored at the axon terminus in Golgi vesicles. The vesicles travel to the axon terminus on a "railroad" constructed of microtubules. When a neuron receives a signal, the Golgi vesicles at the terminus are released from the microtubules and fuse with the axonal membrane, dumping their cargo into the synaptic gap. The neurotransmitters quickly diffuse across the gap and bind to receptors on the dendrite membrane, triggering an electrochemical impulse in the target neuron, thus completing transmission of the signal. This may seem like an awkward way for neurons to signal one another, but the synaptic gap and the use of neurotransmitters are crucial for maintaining the strength of the signal over a network that consists of 100 billion cells.

The *tau* gene and its product have a crucial role in the maintenance of neuronal signal transmission. The *tau* protein is an important component of the microtubule railroad the Golgi vesicles use to reach the axon terminus. A mutation in this gene produces a defective protein, leading to the breakdown of microtubules and a virtual collapse of the

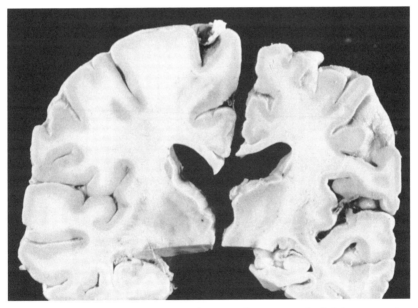

Alzheimer's disease. Sliced sections from two brains. On the left is a normal brain of a 70-year-old. On the right is the brain of a 70-year-old with Alzheimer's disease. The right brain is atrophied, with a loss of cortex and white matter. Alzheimer's disease is a dementing disorder marked by certain brain changes, regardless of the age of onset. *(Biophoto Associates/Photo Researchers, Inc.)*

cell's ability to pass on incoming signals. When a neuron loses its ability to communicate, it is as though it loses its will to live. This phenomenon has been observed in patients suffering from a damaged or severed spinal cord. Peripheral nerves, starved for signals from the CNS, degenerate and die. Similarly, neurons in the brain of an AD patient degenerate and die when signals stop coming in. In this case, however, the loss is

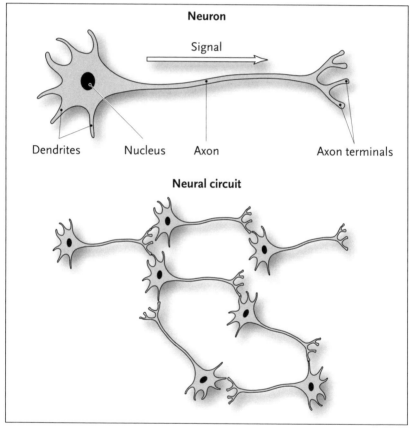

Neural signaling. A neuron receives signals at its dendrites and passes them on to other neurons through its axon. Circuits are constructed with axon terminals making connections with the dendrites of other neurons. The connection between an axon and a dendrite is called a synapse. Circuits in the brain consist of billions of neurons, each forming thousands of synaptic junctions with other neurons. These circuits give us our intellect, our emotions, our ability to see the world, and much more.

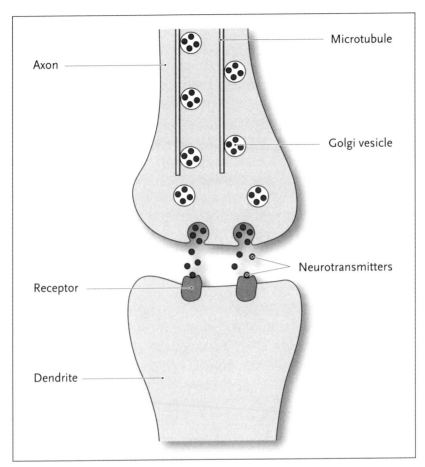

Synaptic junction. Axons and dendrites do not touch each other but are separated by a small gap called the synapse or synaptic junction. A signal is transmitted by the release of small molecules called neurotransmitters that are stored at the axon terminus in Golgi vesicles. Binding of the neurotransmitter to the receptor on the dendrite membrane completes the transmission. The Golgi vesicles travel to the axon terminus on a railroad constructed from microtubules.

more than the movement of an arm or a leg; rather, it affects the core of a person's being.

A second route to the development of AD involves the *app* and *sen* genes. Neurons, like all cells, are covered in a molecular forest called the

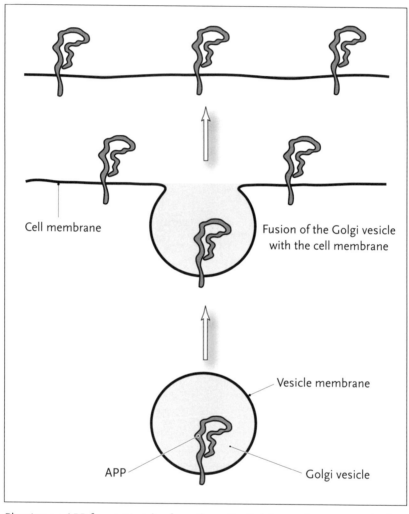

Cell membrane

Fusion of the Golgi vesicle with the cell membrane

Vesicle membrane

APP

Golgi vesicle

Planting an APP forest. Vesicles from the cell's Golgi complex carry amyloid precursor protein (APP) to the cell surface. Fusion of the vesicle membrane with the cell membrane automatically plants APP in the cell membrane.

glycocalyx. This forest consists of a wide variety of glycoproteins, resembling trees, that have many functions: Some are hormone or glucose receptors, others are involved in processing the electrochemical signals generated by neurotransmitters. An important member of a CNS neuron's glycocalyx is the *app* protein (APP), which is believed to be involved in hormonal signal transduction. APP is processed through the Golgi complex and planted on the cell surface by fusion of the Golgi vesicles with the cell membrane.

Neurons suffering from AD fail to process APP properly. This is believed to be due to a mutation in the *sen* gene, resulting in an enzyme that cuts APP in two, producing a truncated APP (tAPP) and a second protein called beta-amyloid. It is not clear whether this happens before or after APP is planted on the cell surface, but the final result is a defective glycocalyx consisting of tAPP and the accumulation of beta-amyloid in the intercellular space. A normal glycocalyx is crucial for a

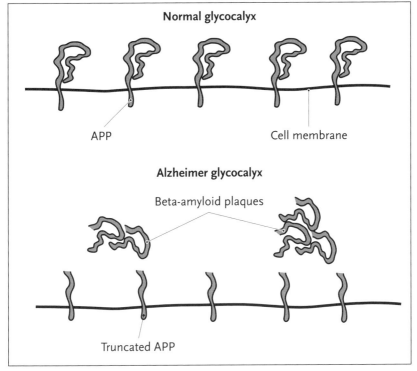

Normal versus Alzheimer-affected glycocalyx. A molecular forest called the glycocalyx covers all cells. An important member of a neuron's glycocalyx is a molecule called amyloid precursor protein (APP). In Alzheimer's disease, APP is cut into two pieces, forming truncated APP and beta-amyloid. The truncated APP (tAPP) remains in the membrane, while the beta-amyloid forms extracellular deposits known as plaques.

cell's survival. In the case of AD, scientists believe the immune system detects the abnormal glycocalyx and orders the cell to commit suicide, in a process known as apoptosis. Thus, whether the onset of AD is through a defective *tau* or *sen* gene, the final outcome—extensive neuronal death—is the same.

At present, there is no way to cure AD, although treatments are being developed to reduce the accumulation of the beta-amyloid, which could be responsible for some of the neuron or circuit damage. Other treatments being planned involve a combination of gene therapy and stem cell transplants to correct the mutated *tau* and *sen* genes and to replace the damaged or dying neuronal population. Experiments show that stem cells injected into damaged rat brains do differentiate into appropriate neurons; whether they make the correct connections, however, is yet to be determined. Given the delicacy of our CNS and the complexity of its circuits, it is likely that such therapies will be extremely difficult to develop.

Arthritis

Although the term literally means "joint inflammation," arthritis really refers to a group of more than 100 rheumatic diseases and conditions that can cause pain, stiffness, and swelling in the joints. If left undiagnosed and untreated, arthritis can cause irreversible damage to the joints. There are two forms of this disease: osteoarthritis and rheumatoid arthritis.

Osteoarthritis, previously known as degenerative joint disease, results from the wear and tear of life. The pressure of gravity and extensive use causes physical damage to the joints and surrounding tissues, leading to pain, tenderness, and swelling. Initially, osteoarthritis is noninflammatory and its onset is subtle and gradual, usually involving one or only a few joints. The joints most often affected are the knee, hip, and hand. Pain is the earliest symptom, usually made worse by repetitive use. Osteoarthritis affects 21 million people in the United States, and the risk of getting it increases with age. Other risk factors include joint trauma, obesity, and repetitive joint use; examples of the latter include pitcher's elbow and the hip-joint difficulties that professional dancers develop as they grow old.

Rheumatoid arthritis is an autoimmune disease that occurs when the body's own immune system mistakenly attacks the synovium (cell lining inside the joint). This chronic, potentially disabling disease causes pain, stiffness, swelling, and loss of function in the joints. The causes of this disease are unclear but could involve a mutation that affects the glycocalyx of the synovium, leading to an immune attack. This mechanism is similar to that proposed for the death of neurons in AD. Rheumatoid arthritis is much rarer than osteoarthritis, affecting about 2 million people in the United States. This disease affects women much more than men (the difference is twofold to threefold) and has led many scientists to suggest it is related to the decline of estrogen levels that occurs in women after menopause. Current treatment involves hormone supplements, but this can place the patient at high risk of developing breast or uterine cancer.

Cancer

Human cancer is primarily an age-related disease that strikes when an individual is 50 years of age or older. The age of the individual and the time element are important largely because the formation of a tumor is a multistep process that takes many years to complete. There are, however, many exceptions to this relationship. Lung cancer, brought on by cigarette smoke, and childhood leukemias are the most notable examples. The chemicals in cigarette smoke are known to accelerate this process, but the factors responsible for cancer acceleration in children are still unclear.

Cancers are age-related because our cells change with time, becoming more susceptible to genetic damage and less capable of dealing with the damage when it does occur. Much of this problem is believed to be due to a reduction in the ability of our immune system to track down and destroy abnormal cells as they appear, giving those cells time to evolve into a potentially lethal cancer.

The increased incidence of cancer as we approach our sixth decade is also coincidental with the onset of sexual senescence in both men and women. It is possible that the hormonal changes that occur during this period contribute to older adults' increased susceptibility to cancer. Age-related hormonal changes include a shift in the ratio of estrogen to testosterone (ET ratio) in both men and women. Young women naturally have a high estrogen/testosterone ratio (a lot of estrogen, very little testosterone), whereas young men have a low estrogen/testosterone ratio (very little estrogen, a lot of testosterone). Estrogen levels drop dramatically in women after menopause, and men show a similar decline in the level of testosterone at a corresponding age. As a consequence, men and women approach a similar ET ratio throughout their sixth to ninth decades, a condition that is thought to influence the rate at which genetic instability occurs. In addition, many scientists believe the shift in the ET ratio is largely responsible for the weakening of the human immune system, leading to the increased occurrence not only of cancer but of many other diseases as well.

Cardiovascular Disease

The most common form of cardiovascular disease is called atherosclerosis, a disease of the arteries that can strike at any age, although it is not a serious threat until we reach our fifth or sixth decades. This is due in part to cellular changes that make the blood vessels less elastic (hardening of the arteries) and weaken the heart muscles, but it is largely due to poor diet and lack of exercise. This disease is characterized by a narrowing of the arteries, caused by the formation of plaques (deposits) containing dead cells and cholesterol. Several factors influence the appearance of plaques, including high levels of cholesterol (and cholesterol precursors, such as triglyceride) in the blood, high blood pressure, and cigarette smoke. The body removes excess cholesterol from the blood using a protein called apolipoprotein E (ApoE). ApoE, encoded by a gene on chromosome 19, binds to cholesterol and delivers it to liver cells, which store it for later use. Mutant ApoE loses the ability to bind to liver receptors, resulting in a buildup of cholesterol in the blood.

A second form of cardiovascular disease affects the coronary arteries, the blood vessels that carry blood to the cardiomyocytes, or heart muscle cells. If coronary arteries become blocked or otherwise damaged, the cardiomyocytes die from lack of oxygen. In serious cases, this can lead to a massive heart attack and death of the patient. In milder cases, damage to the heart is minimal but coronary circulation is insufficient to allow the patient a normal lifestyle. Many treatments are available for cardiovascular disease, including surgical intervention, angioplasty, and gene therapy. But this disease, like diabetes, is largely the result of lifestyle and is not an inevitable consequence of age. A combination of adequate exercise and a healthy diet begun at an early age is the best treatment.

Diabetes

The appearance of life on Earth, more than 3.5 billion years ago, was made possible to a great extent by the presence of glucose in the oceans and the ability of the first cells to use this sugar as a source of energy. To this day, glucose is central to energy metabolism in animals, plants, and microbes. In mammals, defects in glucose metabolism and utilization are caused by a disease known as diabetes.

For microbes, the process of acquiring glucose and extracting its energy is fairly straightforward. Each cell has receptors that import glucose from the environment, and biochemical pathways that break the sugar down to release the energy it contains. One of the pathways, consisting of a coordinated set of enzymes, is called glycolysis (meaning "sugar splitting") and the other is called the Krebs cycle. These pathways convert the sugar's energy to ATP, which is used by all cells as an energy source (see chapter 8).

Glucose metabolism is more complex in humans and other mammals. In mammals, the uptake and utilization of glucose is coordinated by the endocrine system and involves the overall physiological state of the animal to ensure that the system as a whole has an adequate supply of energy. All cells in an animal's body have glucose receptors, but cells do not import glucose unless their receptors are bound to a hormone called insulin, which is produced by the pancreas, a large gland located just below the liver. The pancreas has two types of cells, called α (alpha) and β (beta). The α cells produce digestive enzymes that are secreted directly into the large intestine, and the β cells produce insulin. Glucose in the blood stimulates the β cells to make and release insulin; the amount of insulin released is directly proportional to the concentration of glucose in the blood.

One might wonder why the body bothers with such an indirect mechanism: Why not let each cell take up glucose whenever it can? The short answer to this question is that each cell would take up the glucose—a process that requires energy—whether it needed it or not. Dependence on insulin makes it possible for the endocrine system to regulate the uptake of glucose. For example, if the animal has a meal, but each cell already has plenty of ATP on hand, the endocrine system blocks the uptake of glucose everywhere but the liver, which is instructed to convert the glucose into glycogen, a molecule that serves as a storage depot.

Diabetes destroys the β cells' ability to manufacture insulin, leading to a buildup of glucose in the blood. A chronic elevation of blood glucose levels results in the inappropriate glycosylation (addition of sugar to proteins) of many proteins in the blood, including hemoglobin, the oxygen-carrying protein, as well as many other proteins associated with the cells and tissues. Systemwide protein glycosylation can lead to blindness, heart disease, kidney failure, and neurological disease. This disease is a major health problem in North America, where it causes approximately 500,000 deaths every year. Treatment is very expensive, amounting to about $98 billion annually.

There are two forms of this disease, known as type I and type II diabetes. Type I diabetes is an autoimmune disease, in which the white blood cells attack and destroy the β cells of the pancreas. This form of the disease is sometimes called juvenile diabetes because it occurs predominately in teenagers, although it can strike at any age. Type II diabetes affects older people, usually beginning when they are 50 to 60 years of age. In this case, the disease may be due to a genetic predisposition to short-lived β cells, or it may be due to β cell burnout brought on by a lifelong preference for a diet that is heavy on sweets. This may account for the fact that nearly 80 percent of those suffering from type II diabetes are overweight. At last count, 10 genetic loci were known to be associated with the onset of both types of diabetes.

Osteoporosis

Osteoporosis is a skeletal disorder characterized by weakened bone strength leading to an increased risk of fracture. Bone strength is a function of the mineral content, primarily calcium, and the health of the osteoblasts, the cells that produce the underlying bone matrix.

Bone mineral density (BMD) is a common criterion used to evaluate the onset of this very common disease, which affects more than 20 million people in North America alone. Women are four times more likely to develop osteoporosis than men. One out of every two women and one in eight men over 50 will have an osteoporosis-related fracture in her or his lifetime. Osteoporosis is caused primarily by hormonal changes that affect women and men as they approach their sixth decade. For women, this involves a dramatic drop in estrogen levels at menopause, and for men, a reduction in the levels of testosterone at a comparable age.

Osteoporosis is responsible for more than 1.5 million fractures annually, including 300,000 hip fractures, approximately 700,000 vertebral (spinal) fractures, 250,000 wrist fractures, and more than 300,000 fractures at other sites. In the presence of osteoporosis, fractures can occur from normal lifting and bending, as well as from falls. Osteoporotic fractures, particularly vertebral fractures, are usually associated with crippling pain. Hip fractures are by far the most serious and certainly the most debilitating. One in five patients dies one year following an osteoporotic hip fracture. Fifty percent of those people experiencing a hip fracture will be unable to walk without assistance, and 28 percent will require long-term care.

Current treatments involve calcium and vitamin D supplements (at about 400 to 1,000 IU/day for vitamin D). The preferred calcium source is milk, cheese, or yogurt. Hormone replacement therapy, involving estrogen for women and testosterone for men, has proved to be very effective. However, the effective dose was once believed to be low enough that cancer induction was not a serious concern, but studies concluded in 2003 indicate that this may not be so. Growth hormone is also being tried as a therapy for both men and women to relieve the symptoms of this disease, but the potential for cancer induction is a serious concern. In addition to drug therapies, regular exercise is recommended as a way to prevent the onset of this disease or to minimize its effects once it has started. A sedentary lifestyle has a devastating effect on bone mass because the induction of osteoblasts (bone-forming cells) is known to be dependent on physical activity. Consequently, a lifelong habit of avoiding exercise is believed to be a major risk factor in the onset of osteoporosis.

·4·
ANTIAGING MEDICINE

The treatment of the aging process and of the diseases associated with it is difficult and highly controversial. Many scientists believe there is no such thing as a treatment that will reverse the aging process. Indeed, in 2002, a coalition of 51 gerontologists and biologists took an unprecedented step of publishing a paper that was sharply critical of antiaging medicines and the companies that market them. The following is an excerpt from their position statement:

> There has been a resurgence and proliferation of health care providers and entrepreneurs who are promoting antiaging products and lifestyle changes that they claim will slow, stop or reverse the processes of aging. Even though in most cases there is little or no scientific basis for these claims, the public is spending vast sums of money on these products and lifestyle changes, some of which may be harmful. Scientists are unwittingly contributing to the proliferation of these pseudoscientific antiaging products by failing to participate in the public dialogue about the genuine science of aging research. The purpose of this document is to warn the public against the use of ineffective and potentially harmful antiaging interventions.

The paper gives a thorough overview of what scientists have learned about the aging process and presents detailed arguments against the use of various therapies, particularly those involving hormone supplements, which can be dangerous if used without the supervision of a physician. Most antiaging products, however, are no more dangerous than sunscreens, skin creams, perfumes, and over-the-counter treatments for athlete's foot or acne. Indeed, it is the cosmetics industry that is at the center of this controversy, for it is quick to market any compound that may be used as an antiwrinkle cream or skin exfoliant for what they call the vibrant, youthful look. Whether they have the right to do so is up to governmental agencies, such as the Food and Drug Administration (FDA) in the United States, which oversees the marketing of any compound that claim to have medicinal properties.

To a great extent, the controversy between the gerontologists and the cosmetic industry is reminiscent of the general clash between the scientists who conduct basic biological research, which often discovers potentially useful drugs or therapies, and biotech companies that want to market those products. These two camps frequently have different priorities, but this fact should not interfere with the development of useful medical therapies. In the case of antiaging medicines, some of the drugs, while not reversing the aging process, are effective at alleviating symptoms associated with aging, thus improving the quality of life for millions of people. These drugs, in addition to some of the more controversial therapies, are the subject of this chapter.

Hormone Therapy

Endocrinologists (scientists who study hormones) have known for 30 years that human hormone levels fluctuate with age. Several prominent hormones, such as estrogen, testosterone, thyroid hormone, and growth hormone (GH) decrease dramatically as we reach our sixth decade. One example is the drop in estrogen levels when a women goes through menopause. Men experience a similar, though more gradual, decline in testosterone levels when they reach a comparable age (referred to as andropause). The effect of this decline on human physiology is profound. As described in chapter 3, the problem is not simply a drop in the hormone level but a change in the estrogen/testosterone ratio that occurs in both sexes. A disturbance in this ratio weakens our bones and immune system, and places us at an elevated risk of developing cancer, arthritis, osteoporosis, and other diseases.

Estrogen and testosterone supplementation, which has been a routine medical procedure, is known to reverse the onset of osteoporosis and can alleviate the symptoms of osteoarthritis. The great concern associated with the use of these steroids is their suspected role in cancer induction. In July 2002, NIH released the results of a large hormone therapy trial, involving 16,000 women. The study consisted of two groups, one receiving a combination of estrogen and progesterone, the other a placebo. The results showed an increased risk in the group receiving hormone therapy for breast cancer, heart attacks, and stroke. However, the effect was relatively small. For example, the study suggested that of 10,000 women getting hormone therapy for a year, eight more will develop invasive breast cancer and seven more will have heart attacks compared with a similar group not taking hormones. The benefits would be six fewer cases of colorectal cancer and five fewer hip fractures. The initial response to this study was that women should stop hormone therapy, but many physicians and their patients believe the risks involved are worth it. Moreover, adjusting the hormone dose may make it possible to retain the benefits while reducing the risks.

Human growth hormone (hGH) supplements, advertised by some companies as an antiaging miracle drug, are much more dangerous to use than are the sex steroids. This hormone, as its name implies, promotes growth in children and adolescents, but in a fully mature individual, GH takes care of many other physiological chores, including the daily mobilization of energy reserves and amino acids. The adult chores require much less hGH than would be present in a child or an adolescent. Replacement therapies often produce dangerously high concentrations of hGH in the blood, which can lead to a condition known as acromegaly. This disease, first described in the 1930s, is the result of excessive GH production in an adult, leading to severe disfigurement of the face, hands, and feet, as well as overgrowth of soft tissue, leading to thickening of the skin and visceral organs. In recent years, this disease has occurred in laboratory-bred transgenic salmon containing an extra GH gene. Initially, these fish simply grow faster than their cohorts, but as they approach sexual maturity, they suffer extreme deformities of the head and spine, making it difficult for them to feed and swim (these fish are produced for research purposes only). In 1999 the FDA laid charges against an American company for selling hGH as a medicinal drug and fined the company $50 million.

The hormone thyroxine is also used to alleviate some of the symptoms of old age. Thyroxine, produced by the thyroid gland located at the base of the neck, is important for regulating the activity level of virtually every cell in the body and may be viewed as a tissue growth factor. It is also important for regulating body temperature by stimulating ion pumps, located in cell membranes. The more these pumps work, the more heat they generate. Aging is associated with a decrease in the amount of thyroxine, also referred to as hypothyroidism. Reduced energy level and difficulty keeping warm are the most prominent clinical symptoms of hypothyroidism. Doctors treating this condition routinely prescribe thyroxin supplements, which alleviate some of the symptoms, with few side effects.

Antioxidants

According to the free radical theory of the aging process, antioxidants should help reduce some of the symptoms associated with cellular senescence. Experiments with mice and rats have failed to substantiate this claim. However, there is some evidence suggesting that antioxidants such as vitamin C and E may reduce the threat of Alzheimer's disease by dissolving beta-amyloid plaques (deposits). In addition, research on longevity genes (described in chapter 6) has shown that some of these genes code for proteins that minimize oxidative damage to cells and tissues. This could mean that the failure of previous experiments to substantiate the free radical theory may be the fault of the experimental procedure and, thus, not a true test of the theory.

Caloric Restriction

A starvation diet appears to be the only sure way to increase the mean life span of a mammal. It has been shown to work in mice and rats, and there is at present a very large caloric restriction (CR) study being conducted at the University of Wisconsin on 76 rhesus monkeys. This study will not be concluded until 2005, but the research team released some preliminary results in December 2000. The most notable effect in the CR group is a reduction in the amount of low density lipoprotein (LDL), a macromolecule that is associated with the onset of age-related cardiovascular disease. The CR group has retained a lower body weight and a more youthful appearance but are less active than the control group.

Caloric restriction is important from a theoretical point of view, but it is never likely to form a practical therapy. North Americans in general find it difficult maintaining even modest shifts in eating habits. The typical CR diet, which reduces caloric intake to one-third of normal levels, is not likely to attract a large following. However, CR experiments do highlight the importance of diet on the rate of aging, and this could at least encourage healthier, low-caloric eating habits.

Gene Therapy

Antiaging medicines, such as estrogen or testosterone supplements, do not reverse the aging process, nor do they alleviate all symptoms associated with a loss of those hormones. This is due to the age-related changes that occur in all the cells of the body. Old cells do not respond to hormones the same way they did when they were younger. Hormone receptors in the membranes of every cell change with time, as does the translation machinery that uses mRNA to synthesize proteins. Success with treating age-related diseases will always be limited until the health of each cell in the body can be restored—a big job, but not inconceivable. Cloning technology has shown that it is possible to reprogram a highly differentiated nucleus to assume the functional status of an undifferentiated embryonic cell. Nuclear transfer, the method used to clone Dolly the sheep, is really a form of cellular rejuvenation. When a nucleus from an adult cell is placed inside an enucleated egg, the environment of the egg reprograms and rejuvenates the old nucleus. Factors exist in the cytoplasm of the egg cell that are capable of doing this, and with the human genome project complete, it will soon be possible to identify them all.

The great challenge will be learning how to reset the clock for each of the 200 cell types that make up the human body. Data from the genome project, coupled with the expression arrays described in chapter 1, will make it possible to determine the expression profile for every one of our 30,000 genes. Resetting the clock will involve adjusting the expression profile for every cell with gene therapy. When this is accomplished, true antiaging therapies will finally be available.

·5·
THE HISTORY OF GERONTOLOGY

Gerontology is a branch of the biological sciences devoted to the study of the aging process and its effects on cells and organisms. Philosophers and scientists have been interested in this subject for thousands of years, but this history will be confined to the modern era, extending back no further than the late 1800s. The history of gerontology, like many other branches of biological research, may be divided into four epochs. The first, covering the early years, began around 1870 with the invention of the compound microscope and ended in the 1950s. The second epoch began with the discovery of the DNA double helix in 1952 and extended to the early 1970s. The third epoch began with the introduction of recombinant DNA technology in 1973, ending in the early 1990s. The current epoch, known as the postgenomic era, began with the formation of a genome sequencing consortium in 1990 and continues to the present day.

Gerontological research has always been driven by the same questions: Why do we grow old? Why do we change with time? Can the effects of age be reversed? Gerontologists have tried to answer these questions using a variety of techniques, but with the approach of the third and fourth epochs, the questions became more numerous, more specific, and much more complex.

The Early Years

In 1868 the German physicist Ernst Abbe perfected the design of the compound microscope and in so doing made it possible for scientists to study the structure and function of individual cells in a way that was never before possible. While many microbiologists of the time concentrated on studying the link between disease and microbes, many others began studying the life cycle of bacteria and protozoa in the hope it would shed some light on the aging process. These studies were descriptive in nature; that is, the researcher observed the behavior of the cells and recorded it without subjecting the system to experimental procedures that would modulate the rate of the aging process.

In 1882, August Weismann, a German embryologist, proposed the first theory of senescence (the process of growing old) that tried to link life span to natural selection. Weismann argued that the termination of life may have a selective advantage, and that there is a connection between a species' life span and its ecological niche, body size, and intelligence. During this same period, German chemists were developing the first biochemical techniques that allowed Hans Krebs to work out the cyclic details of energy metabolism that now bear his name (the Krebs cycle, also known as the citric acid cycle). The new biochemical techniques were used by chemists to begin cataloging the many molecules of the cell, and by the time the citric acid cycle had been worked out in 1937, DNA had been identified and localized to the cell nucleus. During the last three decades of the 1800s, European scientists, most notably Anton Schneider, Paul Erlich, Santiago Ramón y Cajal, and Camillo Golgi, were developing special dyes and procedures that could be used to stain cells, in order to study better the nucleus, cell division, and cytoplasmic organelles, thus giving birth to histochemistry and histology.

Thus it was that light microscopy, biochemistry, histochemistry, and histology became the basic tool kit for gerontologists during the early years of scientific research in this field. Scientists at that time believed they had all the techniques that were needed to fully understand the structure and the function of cells and animals. They were only partly right. The techniques of that day made it possible for scientists to gain a basic understanding of cell structure and, to some extent, how that structure changes with time, but they learned very little about the functional significance of those changes or how their knowledge could be used to form a physiological theory of the aging process. Elie Metchnikoff, winner of the 1908 Nobel Prize for his work on the human immune system, attempted to form such a theory by suggesting that lactic-acid bacteria (such as *Bacillus acidophilus*) in the digestive tract could prolong life by preventing putrefaction (decay). He noted that Bulgarian villagers, who eat large quantities of curded milk and yogurt, were known for their longevity. Other scientists of the time believed the secret of long life depended on hormones and, in particular, claimed that an extract of dog endocrine glands could reverse the signs of age. Studies such as these make it clear that the early gerontologists had only vague notions about the mechanisms of cellular senescence.

DNA Structure Inspires New Theories

On April 25, 1953, James Watson and Francis Crick published their classic paper on DNA in the journal *Nature.* Their paper, titled "A Structure for Deoxyribose Nuclei Acid," not only proposed a structural model for the DNA molecule but also showed how DNA could store a genetic code, specifying a unique protein, and how that code could be duplicated, in a process now known as DNA replication. Watson and Crick were also the first to propose the existence of a molecular intermediary (messenger RNA) between DNA and protein synthesis, and special adaptor molecules (transfer RNA) that were part of the protein synthesis machinery. By 1966, using synthetic messenger RNAs, other scientists had worked out the complete genetic code, thereby establishing the one-gene-one-protein hypothesis and describing the functional relationships between replication, transcription, and translation.

Gerontologists of the second epoch quickly realized that the genetic code and the events of protein synthesis gave them, for the first time, testable theories of the aging process. The first, proposed by Deham Harman in 1956, was the free radical theory, and the second, proposed by Leslie Orgel in 1963, was the error catastrophe theory. Both of these theories (described in chapter 2) suggest that aging is caused by errors in biosynthesis, due either to free radicals or to inherent error frequencies associated with transcription and translation. In either case, according to the theories, the result is a buildup of dysfunctional proteins that damage normal cellular functions, thus reducing cell viability with time. The error catastrophe theory was first tested on bacteria, experimental organisms introduced to gerontology during the early years. To further test this theory and the free radical theory, gerontologists of the second epoch began using baker's yeast (*Saccharomyces cerevisiae*), the housefly (*Musca domestica*), the fruit fly (*Drosophila melanogaster*), the rat, and the mouse (*mus musculus*). Experiments on all these organisms, though offering some support for the free radical theory, failed to substantiate the original formulation of the error catastrophe theory.

However, many investigators were quick to realize that even though induced errors in protein synthesis had no effect on the rate of aging, other errors, involving replication or the repair of the DNA molecule, could still be an important, if not primary, cause of the aging process. Testing the revised catastrophe theory required detailed information about the gene, but at the time, there was no way to sequence DNA or to infer the sequence of messenger RNA. Throughout the 1960s, physicists were busy perfecting the electron microscope, which offered unparalleled resolution of cellular organelles and tissue ultrastructure. Consequently, many gerontologists turned their attention to refining the structural and biochemical analysis of age-related changes that was begun by scientists of the first epoch. These studies, carried out on the housefly, *Drosophila*, and mouse, introduced methods for modulating the life span of the organism. The life span of houseflies, for example, was tripled when they were reared in tiny cages that minimized flight activity. Caloric restriction was also introduced, which could extend the life span of a mouse by 30 to 40 percent. Finally, with extensive genetic data available for *Drosophila*, many researchers conducted studies on long-lived or short-lived mutants in an attempt to correlate their life span with changes at the cellular or biochemical level. Although the research in the second epoch used more powerful techniques than were available during the first epoch, the results were still largely descriptive in nature and generally fell far short of achieving a deeper understanding of the aging process.

Recombinant Technology Revolutionizes the Field

In 1973, Paul Berg, a professor of biochemistry at Stanford University, produced the first recombinant DNA molecule, consisting of a piece of mammalian DNA joined to a bacterial plasmid (a bacterial minichromosome). Bacteria have a natural tendency to take up plasmids from the medium they are growing in; once they do, the plasmid DNA, with any insert it may contain, is replicated along with the bacterial chromosome each time the cell divides. This proliferation of a segment of DNA is called amplification.

To amplify a mammalian gene, bacteria are coaxed to take up a recombinant plasmid in a small test tube containing a special medium, after which they are transferred to a large flask containing nutrient broth and allowed to grow for 24 hours. By the end of the culturing period, the amount of cloned insert has increased more than a million-fold. In 1977, Fred Sanger, a professor at Cambridge University, and Walter Gilbert, a professor at Harvard, developed methods for sequencing DNA. The production of recombinant clones, combined with the new sequencing technology, made it possible to isolate any gene and to produce enough of it for sequencing and expression studies (see chapter 8 for more details).

Expression studies observe the transcription of a gene to produce messenger RNA (mRNA) and the resulting translation of mRNA into protein. Because most mRNA is automatically translated into protein, conducting an expression study involves determining the amount of mRNA being produced by a specific gene. The information gained by doing so is extremely important because all cellular processes are ultimately controlled by the differential expression of various genes. Some genes in some cells always stay off, whereas some are always on (constitutive expression), and some turn on or off as conditions demand (regulative expression). One theory of aging suggests that the aging process is caused by subtle disruptions in the normal control of gene expression. At first, gerontologists tried to test this assumption by examining the protein products of translation with two-dimensional (2-d) protein electrophoresis, a technology introduced in 1977. But 2-d electrophoresis can detect only a few hundred proteins; a typical cell is capable of producing thousands of different proteins. Despite its limitations, many studies were conducted with this procedure throughout the 1980s on wild-type (normal) or mutant *Drosophila*. The hope was that electrophoresis would show that old animals were completely missing a protein present in young animals or that a new protein would appear in old animals that might be responsible for the age-related changes. But no such results were ever obtained, at least not on a consistent basis. The studies failed to show a consistent change in any of the proteins that could be visualized with this technique. The animals were clearly aging, but they seemed to be making the same proteins when they were old as when they were young.

Still investigating whether the absence or presence of a given protein influenced aging, expression studies conducted in the third epoch of gerontology research turned to recombinant technology, instead of protein electrophoresis. With recombinant technology, it is theoretically possible to study the mRNA expression of every gene in the cell. Consequently, gerontologists of the third epoch conducted a large number of expression studies involving genes coding for globin, actin, liver enzymes, microtubules, apolipoprotein (a protein that carries lipids in the blood), brain- and kidney-specific proteins, and several oncogenes. In most cases the choice of which gene to study was an equal mix of educated guess and common practicality. If an investigator had a hunch that a particular liver enzyme was responsible for some aspect of cellular aging, the expression of the gene could be studied, but only if it had already been cloned (the clone, as explained in chapter 8, serves as a probe to localize and quantify the mRNA). Since no one at the time had a clear idea of which genes were responsible for the aging process, virtually any gene for which a probe was available made a good candidate for an expression study.

It was during this epoch that investigators demonstrated the striking age-related decline in the expression of the growth hormone (GH) gene in rats, which was later confirmed in the mouse and human. However, other expression studies, carried out primarily on rat, *Drosophila,* and housefly tissues did not produce the striking results that most scientists were expecting. The expression of some genes was shown to increase with age while others decreased, but there was no obvious connection to cellular senescence. Even worse, the expression of some genes was shown to decrease with age in the rat but not in *Drosophila* or the mouse, and since the aging process should be similar for all animals, those genes could not be the cause of a universal aging mechanism. When all expression studies were taken together, there appeared to be a general decline in the rate of gene expression with age and, with the exception of GH expression, no clear support for any single theory of the aging process.

Those scientists interested in chromatin structure and the role it plays in regulating gene expression adopted a different approach to the study of the aging process. Eukaryote chromosomes are a complex of DNA and proteins, called histones, that are arranged on the DNA like beads on a string. Each bead, consisting of several different kinds of histone, is called a nucleosome. This complex of DNA and histones is known as chromatin. The histones are essential for packing up the chromosomes in preparation for cell division. Phosphorylating the nucleosomes (adding phosphate groups to the proteins) is like releasing a stretched rubber band: The chromosome contracts to form a compact structure that is 10,000 times shorter than the bare piece of DNA. Just as a suitcase makes it possible for us to take our clothes on a trip, histones and the chromatin structure they produce make it possible for the cell to package its genes in preparation for cell division (see the eukaryote cell primer in chapter 8).

Chromatin compaction, or condensation, is also used during interphase (the period between cell divisions) to help manage the chromosomes. It is also one mechanism for controlling gene expression. The packing ratio of interphase chromatin (condensed length divided by

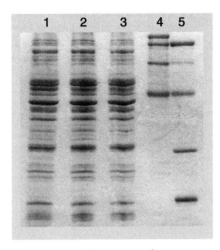

Protein electrophoresis. In this procedure, proteins are extracted from cells of interest and then fractionated by electrophoresis on a polyacrylamide gel. After the gel is stained, or exposed to X-ray film, the proteins appear as bands. In the example shown, approximately 30 different proteins (bands) have been identified. Lanes 1 to 3 are proteins extracted from housefly flight muscle at 1, 4, and 8 days of age. Lanes 4 and 5 are size markers that decrease in size from top to bottom. In a different form of this procedure, called two-dimensional protein electrophoresis, the proteins appear as spots over the face of the gel. Two-dimensional protein gels have a higher resolution and can detect about 1,000 different proteins, but this is still much less than the more than 20,000 proteins a typical animal cell can produce. (Dr. Joseph Panno)

relaxed length) is about 1:1,000 overall, but there are highly condensed regions where it can be as low as 1:10,000. This variation in the density of the chromatin accounts for the blotchy appearance that most inter-phase nuclei have. Areas of the nucleus that are very dark represent highly compacted chromatin, whereas the lighter regions contain chromatin in a more relaxed state. At the molecular level, chromatin condensation is an extremely dynamic process that is used to close down single genes or whole neighborhoods consisting of hundreds of genes. The mechanism by which this occurs is fairly straightforward: Highly condensed chromatin blocks the transcription machinery, so it cannot get access to the gene.

Many gerontologists of the third epoch studied chromatin condensation as a function of age. These studies were either biochemical or they relied on computerized histochemistry. The biochemical analysis depended on the fact that uncondensed chromatin is easy to dissociate (i.e., it is easy to separate the histones from the DNA) in certain buffers, whereas highly condensed chromatin is either very difficult to dissociate or does not dissociate at all. Studies such as these invariably showed that chromatin became more condensed with age. Consequently, condensed chromatin was believed to be responsible for the age-related reduction in transcriptional activity. Computerized histochemical analysis of intact nuclei supported the biochemical results and, in addition, provided a way to visualize the progressive condensation of cell nuclei. Scientists produced a model of this progressive condensation by analyzing the condensation pattern over the surface of the nucleus and then, with the aid of computer algorithms, selecting nuclei that best represent the young and old groups.

In 1987, to better facilitate the interpretation of aging research data, the American National Institute of Aging (NIA) launched the Bio-markers of Aging Project to identify biological signs, or biomarkers, in human subjects that best characterize the aging process. Biomarkers, which include the performance of the cardiovascular system, blood insulin levels, blood pressure, and several other factors, are usually a better measure of an organism's aging rate than is chronological age (see the accompanying table).

The third epoch was a productive period for gerontological research that provided many insights into the mechanisms controlling

BIOMARKERS OF NORMAL AGING[1]	
Biomarker	**Change with Age**
Arteries	Flexibility decreases
Blood pressure	Increases
Body fat	Increases, but can be prevented with exercise
Brain	Some neurons lost; basic functions remain intact, but short-term memory declines
Cholesterol	Increases, but can be prevented with exercise and diet
Dehydroepiandrosterone (DHEA)[2]	Decreases
Hearing	Detection of high frequencies is lost
Heart	Thickness of ventricular wall increases
Insulin	Blood concentration increases
Kidneys	Reduction in urine output
Lungs	Vital capacity[3] declines by about 40 percent
Vision	Ability to focus close up is lost, night vision becomes poor, and ability to detect moving objects is impaired.

[1]Normal, or successful, aging occurs in the absence of such diseases as Alzheimer's or Parkinson's.
[2]DHEA is a precursor of the sex hormones estrogen and testosterone.
[3]Vital capacity is the maximum amount of air inspired with each breath.

the aging process. However, most scientists began to realize that the final assault on this very difficult problem would require more DNA sequence data to expand the expression profile for the organisms under study. Indeed, it became clear that what was needed was the complete genomic sequence for humans and for all organisms for which age-related studies were under way.

The Postgenomic Era

An international genome sequencing consortium was formed in 1990 to sequence human, bacteria, yeast, nematode (*Caenorhabditis elegans,* or simply *C. elegans*), *Drosophila,* and mouse genomes. This project was initiated by the United States Department of Energy and the National Research Council and is coordinated by the Human Genome Organization (HUGO). The principal consortium members include the United States, United Kingdom, France, Germany, Japan, and China. Sequencing of the human genome was completed in early 2003, and it is expected that the genomes of the other organisms will be completed by 2005 (for additional information, see chapter 8).

In 1993 the American National Institute of Aging (NIA) started a program to identify longevity genes in yeast, nematode, *Drosophila,* and mice. This program provided research funding for scientists at NIA, as well as other scientists working in university laboratories around the country. The main interest of this program is single-gene mutants that may be used to identify genes and physiological factors that favor longevity in all animal species. These include the insulin-like signaling pathway, stress resistance, and most recently, chromosome and nuclear architecture. The ultimate goal of this program is to use information gathered from lower animals to identify longevity genes in humans.

In addition to financial support, the NIA program and the genome sequencing consortium provided encouragement and focus to the gerontological community. Research focus came in two forms. First, by settling on just four research organisms, different research groups could easily compare results. Gerontology of previous epochs was carried out to a great extent on houseflies and rats, neither of which are genetically defined (i.e., mutants have not identified or characterized). The four organisms chosen by NIA are well characterized genetically, and there are many long- and short-lived mutants available that greatly expedite aging research. Second, aging research shifted from projects aimed at testing one of the many theories of the aging process to a narrower, thus more practical approach involving the search for longevity genes. This was done by selecting for long-lived individuals or by searching for naturally occurring short-lived mutants. In some cases, exposing the animals to chemical mutagens generated short-lived mutants. There is also a great deal of interest in a human disease known as Werner's syndrome that is characterized by a greatly accelerated rate of aging. Individuals suffering from this disease age so rapidly that they appear to be in their 70s or 80s by the time they are 10 years old.

The great value of the sequencing consortium in the effort to identify aging genes lies in the fact that all the organisms under study, including humans, share a common cellular and genetic heritage. Thus, if a longevity gene is discovered in *Drosophila,* its homolog (a gene having a similar or identical sequence) can be identified in humans simply by searching the human database for a gene that matches the *Drosophila* sequence. Research of this kind (described more extensively in the next chapter) is bringing us closer to identifying the physiological processes and molecular mechanisms that are important for longevity. Reversal of the aging process, and treatment of its clinical symptoms, will become a practical reality after all the genes controlling these processes have been identified and their functions clearly defined.

.6.

THE SEARCH FOR
LONGEVITY GENES

Aging research throughout the first three epochs of gerontology was primarily concerned with describing general aspects of the process covering all levels of biological organization, from the molecular to the organismal. The data collected spawned a large number of theories (covered in chapter 2) touching on all aspects of cellular structure and function, as well as changes that may occur at the physiological level. Although these theories were crucial for producing advances in the discipline, they failed to produce a clear picture of fundamental mechanisms responsible for the aging process. However, beginning in 1993 with the NIA program to isolate aging genes, there has been a great surge in the genetic analysis of aging and a better understanding of the molecular mechanisms, signaling pathways, and physiological processes that promote longevity.

Thus, with the beginning of the current epoch and the launching of comprehensive genome sequencing projects, the goal of gerontology shifted to the identification and characterization of genes that promote longevity. Despite their name, longevity genes were not always selected by evolutionary forces to give an organism a long life span. Quite the contrary, since some of these genes, when functioning normally, limit the life span. It's only after being mutated and made dysfunctional that they increase the organism's life span. This type of longevity gene is said to be a negative regulator of life span because their normal function is to limit an organism's life span. Other longevity genes are said to be positive regulators because expression (or overexpression) of these genes increases the life span.

The normal life span of an organism is produced by a complex mix of positive and negative regulator genes that seem to produce the optimum—not necessarily the longest—life span that best fits the organism's size, metabolic rate, and activity level, and its position in the grander theater of predator-prey relationships. The search for longevity genes in yeast, nematode, *Drosophila,* mice, and humans has lead to a much clearer picture of the mechanisms controlling the aging process. It has also shed light on how those mechanisms can be modulated to fine-tune an organism's life span to maximize the survival, not of the individual, but of the species to which it belongs. Gerontology researchers expect, however, that a clear understanding of all longevity genes will provide a way of reversing or stalling the signs of age in humans.

Yeast

Yeast are unicellular organisms that divide at regular intervals and, as a population, are immortal. Each cell begins as a mother cell that pro-

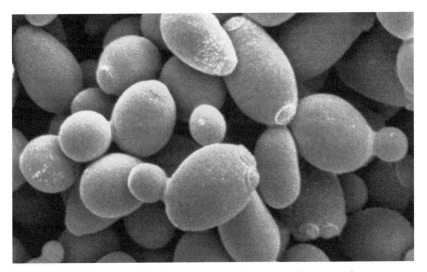

Researchers in the search for longevity genes have used yeast, such as *Saccharomyces cerevisiae.* This image shows several of the cells in the process of cell division by budding, which produces a daughter cell that is initially smaller than the mother cell. *(SciMAT/Photo Researchers, Inc.)*

duces a daughter cell each time it divides, but the mother cell ages with each cell division; thus its life span is limited to a finite number of cell divisions, after which it dies, while the daughter cells continue on for the same finite number cell divisions. The measure of the yeast life span is thus the number of divisions of the mother cell before it dies, not the amount time it has lived. The identification of longevity genes in yeast provided the first comprehensive list of physiological processes that are now believed to control the aging process. These processes are metabolic control, resistance to stress, gene dysregulation, and the maintenance of genetic stability.

The first longevity gene, called *lag-1* (longevity assurance gene number 1), was isolated from yeast by Dr. S. Michel Jazwinski and his team at Louisiana State University in 1994. Since that time, 14 additional longevity genes have been identified in yeast (see the table for a partial list). The *lag-1* protein (LAG-1) is located in the membrane of the endoplasmic reticulum and is involved in the production of glycolipids (by convention, gene names are written in lowercase italic, whereas the protein product is written in uppercase roman). Glycolipids are an important component of the glycocalyx, a molecular "forest" that covers the surface of all cells. The glycocalyx is essential for cell-to-cell communication and contains many receptors that regulate a host of cellular functions. Many glycolipids are involved in signaling pathways that regulate growth, stress resistance, and apoptosis. LAG-1 is a positive regulator of life span, and while the mechanism by which it influences life span is unclear, a mutation in this gene could reduce the cell's ability to cope with stress, to block proliferation, or to induce apoptosis.

All eukaryotes have an intracellular signaling pathway, known as the retrograde response, that serves to coordinate mitochondrial function with the expression of mitochondrial genes in the cell nucleus. Although mitochondria have their own genome, most of the Krebs cycle enzymes (all of which function inside the mitochondrion) are coded for by the cellular genome. The rate at which these genes are transcribed depends on how badly the mitochondria need the enzymes. During periods of stress, caused by high temperatures or an unfavorable environment, mitochondria are extremely active. All enzymes have a relatively short life span, and during periods of extreme activity, they must be replaced more frequently. Ensuring that the mitochondria always have enough Krebs cycle enzymes is the main function of the retrograde response, a process that is regulated by two other longevity genes, called *ras-1* and *ras-2*. Mutations in either or both of these genes eliminate the retrograde response, thus abolishing the cell's ability to deal with stress of the kind described. Consequently, the cell does not receive sufficient amounts of ATP, the main energy source, at a time when it needs it the most, resulting in cellular damage and early death. Overexpression of *ras-2* can completely abolish the negative effect on life span of chronic heat stress. Yeast demonstrating natural thermotolerance early in life invariably have longer life spans than is normal.

Genetic dysregulation with age has been observed in yeast that lose transcriptional silencing of genes in heterochromatic regions of the genome (i.e., genes in highly condensed regions are supposed to be turned off). Active regions of the genome are associated with chromatin that is acetylated; that is, the histones are modified with the addition of acetyl groups, as though to mark the region as being transcriptionally active. Two yeast longevity genes, *rpd-3* and *hda-1,* code for enzymes called deacetylases that remove the acetyl groups, thus converting chromatin from an active to an inactive configuration. Normal aging in yeast is associated with the continued expression of genes that are supposed to be silent, presumably because of a loss of *rpd-3* and *hda-1* activity. A third gene, called *sir-2,* is also responsible for gene silencing, but its mechanism is not clear. Damage to any of these silencing genes is responsible for an age-related dysregulation of the ribosomal RNA genes, resulting in an excessive production of ribosomal RNA that is not balanced by the synthesis of ribosomal proteins. The consequence is the assembly of defective ribosomes and a reduction in the efficiency of protein synthesis.

Genetic stability, the fourth major process affected by the aging process, is maintained by a host of nuclear proteins and enzymes that repair DNA damage and by many other proteins that are needed for accurate replication. One such enzyme, called a helicase, is encoded by the *sgs-1* gene. The function of a helicase is to unwind the DNA helix in preparation for replication. Mutation of this gene leads to the corruption of many genes during replication and is associated with accelerated aging.

YEAST LONGEVITY GENES	
Gene	**Known or Proposed Function**
lag-1	The *lag-1* protein product (LAG-1) regulates traffic between the endoplasmic reticulum and Golgi complex and is required for the construction of a normal glycocalyx. The aging mechanism is unclear but may involve cell-surface (mediated by the glycocalyx) signaling that influences growth, stress resistance, and apoptosis.
ras-1	Its product is responsible for regulating the stress response.
ras-2	Its product regulates mitochondrial retrograde response, participates in the regulation of the stress response, and is necessary for genetic stability.
rpd-3	Its product is a histone deacetylase that is needed for proper gene silencing and regulation.
hda-1	Its product is another histone deacetylase that regulates silencing of ribosomal RNA genes.
sir-2	Regulates ribosomal RNA genes.
sgs-1	Its protein product codes for a DNA helicase, required for DNA replication. This gene is homologous to the human *wrn* gene, which, when mutated, greatly accelerates the rate of aging.

Nematode

A nematode is a very small round worm that inhabits the soil and sometimes the digestive tracts of mammals. Mammalian parasite nematodes are known as pinworms. The nematode *C. elegans* is a popular research organism among developmental biologists and gerontologists. Several longevity genes have been identified in *C. elegans,* most of which are involved in an insulin-like signaling pathway (see table). At the head of this pathway is the insulin-like receptor, encoded by the gene *daf-2.*

The DAF-2 pathway mediates growth and proliferation signals necessary for the active lifestyle of an adult nematode. Mutation of *daf-2* shifts the entire physiology of the animal from active behavior to something resembling hibernation in mammals. Hibernation behavior in nematodes is known as a diapause state. Nematode diapause is characterized by a shift from active glucose metabolism (i.e., burning calories) to storage functions, such as the deposit of fat. The animal's activity level drops, and the life span is increased by nearly 80 percent. Thus *daf-2* is a negative regulator of life span; it is an example of the kind of gene that limits life span as a result of maximizing activity level and metabolic performance. The effects observed in *daf-2* mutants are very similar to the response of mammals to hibernation or caloric restriction. The products of other nematode longevity genes, such as *age-1, daf-18, akt-1,* and *daf-16,* transduce the signal received by the DAF-2 receptor protein (e.g., the *age-1* protein conveys the signal from the DAF-2 receptor to the cell cytoplasm). Consequently, a mutation in any of these genes will lead to the diapause state and extended life span.

A second pathway has been identified that affects nematode longevity. The *daf-12* gene codes for a steroid hormone receptor that is linked to a pathway that appears to regulate the stress response. Indeed, this pathway specifies resistance to heat, ultraviolet radiation, and oxidative stress. Accordingly, *daf-12* is a positive regulator of life span. A mutation in *daf-12* or in *ctl-1,* a component of the pathway, shortens life span.

Fruit Fly

The fruit fly *Drosophila melanogaster* is a popular research organism. During the 1980s, researchers managed to isolate long-lived *Drosophila* through selective breeding. These flies showed a greater metabolic capacity and enhanced resistance to stress initiated by heat, desiccation, and ethanol vapors. In addition, they have higher activities of antioxidative enzymes, they are more efficient at utilizing nutrients, and they have enhanced stores of lipid and glycogen. Many of these features are held in common with long-lived nematodes and yeast.

Direct support for the free radical theory of the aging process came with the isolation and characterization of *sod-1,* the gene coding for superoxide dismutase (see table). Transgenic fruit flies overexpressing *sod-1* live longer than normal and suffer much less oxidative damage

CAENORHABDITIS ELEGANS LONGEVITY GENES	
Gene	**Known or Proposed Function**
daf-2	Its product codes for an insulin-like cell-membrane receptor (DAF-2). Disrupting this pathway extends life span.
age-1 / daf-23	These genes code for two kinases, directly linked to the DAF-2 signaling pathway.
daf-18	The protein product is on the DAF-2 pathway, downstream from the *age-1/daf-23* products.
akt-1 / akt-2	The products of these genes are on the DAF-2 pathway, downstream from *daf-18*.
daf-16	Its product, DAF-16, is a multifunction factor that is activated by the DAF-2 and DAF-12 pathways. Loss of function promotes a "hibernation" response, involving the storage of fat and glycogen that extends life span.
daf-12	Its product codes for a steroid hormone receptor (DAF-12) that is linked to a pathway that is important in stress resistance. A mutation in this gene shortens life span.
ctl-1	The protein product is a cytoplasmic enzyme (catalase) on the DAF-12 stress-resistance pathway.

induced by free radicals. Interestingly, overexpression of *sod-1* in motorneurons alone is sufficient to nearly double the mean life span of these animals. Overexpression of another gene, *mth*, also increases life span. The *mth* protein product, called methuselah, is a cell-surface receptor that is linked to a pathway that regulates the stress response.

The retrograde response (already described in the discussion on yeast longevity) involving traffic between the cell nucleus, cytoplasm, and the mitochondria is also involved in *Drosophila* aging. The *indy* (*i'm not dead yet*) gene codes for a mitochondrial membrane protein involved in transport of Krebs cycle intermediates. A mutation in the *indy* gene blocks import of these compounds, with an effect similar to caloric restriction—a near doubling of life span. Insulin and insulin

DROSOPHILA LONGEVITY GENES	
Gene	**Known or Proposed Function**
indy	Its product codes for a mitochondrial membrane protein involved in transport of Krebs cycle intermediates. The loss of function increases life span by reducing the availability of nutrients (caloric restriction).
sod-1	The protein product is superoxide dismutase (SOD). Overexpression increases life span by enhanced inactivation of free radicals.
mth	Its product codes for a cell-membrane receptor called methuselah, which enhances the stress response, thus increasing life span.
chico	The protein product, CHICO, is similar to mammalian insulin. Loss of function increases life span through caloric restriction.
inr	Its product codes for the CHICO receptor. Lose of function has the same effect as a chico mutation. This receptor is very similar to the nematode DAF-2 receptor.
sugar baby	The protein product is a maltose permease. Overexpression increases life span by shifting metabolism away from glucose, thus invoking partial caloric restriction.

receptors modulate life span in *Drosophila,* much as they do in nematodes. The *Drosophila* genes *chico* and *inr* (*insulin receptor*) encode an insulin protein and insulin receptor very similar to those found in nematodes and mammals. Mutations in *chico* or *inr* have the same physiological effects as described for the *daf-2* gene in nematodes. The *sugar baby* gene achieves a similar though muted effect on life span. This gene codes for a maltose permease, an enzyme that enhances the uptake of maltose into cells. Overexpression of this gene shifts the animal's physiology away from glucose utilization, thus mimicking the effects of caloric restriction. In this case, the increase in life span is about 20 percent, compared with the more than 80 percent increase observed in *inr* mutants.

Mouse

The most consistent way to extend the life span of a mammal is by caloric restriction. Such experiments (described in chapter 2) have extended the life spans of mice and rats by up to 50 percent. Moreover, these calorie-restricted animals show similar metabolic responses observed in yeast, nematodes, and fruit flies, including resistance to stress. In addition, calorie-restricted rodents show a postponement of age-related diseases, such as cancer, and have an increased lifetime metabolic capacity. These changes, like the hibernation response in nematodes and flies, are due to more efficient utilization of glucose and a shift toward deposit of fat and glycogen.

Three mouse genes have been identified that, when mutated, extend life span in a manner similar to caloric restriction (see table). The gene *prop-1* ("prophet of *pit-1*") codes for a protein that regulates another gene, *pit-1,* that codes for a pituitary-specific transcription factor. Mutation of *prop-1* or *pit-1* leads to developmental arrest of the pituitary gland, thus drastically reducing the normal levels of growth-inducing hormones such growth hormone (GH) and thyroid hormone (TH). In the absence of these hormones, cells cannot utilize glucose or amino acids to promote growth and maturation. Consequently, *prop-1* mutants are dwarves, but they have an extended life span. The consequence of this mutation is the same as if the animals were raised on a calorie-restricted diet even while in the womb.

A second type of longevity gene has been identified in mice. This is the $p66^{shc}$ gene, which codes for a component of a signaling pathway that regulates the stress response and apoptosis. As with the other positive longevity genes already described, overexpression of this gene increases life span, while animals possessing a normally expressed $p66^{shc}$ have shorter life spans.

Human

Identification of longevity genes in lower organisms has stimulated a search for similar genes in the human genome. The human homolog of yeast *lag-1* has already been cloned and is located on chromosome 19. Although the sequence homology is low, it can replace the yeast gene,

MOUSE LONGEVITY GENES	
Gene	**Known or Proposed Function**
prop-1	The protein product is regulator of a pituitary-specific transcription factor (PIT-1). Inactivation leads to poor development of the pituitary and production of pituitary hormones, particularly growth hormone. Mutated *prop-1* increases life span by about 50 percent.
pit-1	This gene codes for PIT-1, a protein transcription factor. The inactivation of *pit-1* has the same effect as a *prop-1* mutation.
p66^{shc}	The protein product is a component of a signal transduction pathway that makes cells resistant to apoptosis and oxidative stress.

where it performs a longevity function. Consequently, human *lag-1* may be thought of as a human longevity gene, although much work is needed to confirm its function in humans.

Perhaps the most striking similarity between longevity genes in humans and lower organisms is the yeast *sgs-1* gene and the human *wrn* gene. The *sgs-1* gene codes for a helicase and, when mutated, can accelerate the aging process. Werner's syndrome, described previously, is a disease in humans that is also associated with accelerated aging. The gene responsible for this disease, called *wrn*, has been identified. The protein product of the *wrn* gene is a helicase, not the same helicase encoded by the *sgs-1* gene, but a member of the same family, possessing a similar function. Mutations in these two genes provide dramatic evidence in support of the connection between life span and genetic stability.

Summary

The search for longevity genes has identified four physiological processes that influence life span. They are metabolic control, resistance to stress, gene dysregulation, and genetic stability. Evidence supporting the involvement of metabolic control comes from the roles of *lag-1* in yeast, *daf-2* in nematodes, *indy* and *sod-1* in *Drosophila*, and *prop-1* in mice. Resistance to stress is a function of several longevity genes, such as *ras-2*, *daf-12*, *mth*, and *p66^{shc}*. Gene dysregulation, as a mechanism of aging, has been clearly demonstrated in yeast with the isolation of three histone deacytlase genes, *rpd-3*, *hda-1*, and *sir-2*. Finally, the relationship between genetic stability and life span is indicated by the effects of *sgs-1* mutants in yeast and the human disease known as Werner's syndrome, which is associated with accelerated aging and is caused by the gene *wrn*, a homolog of *sgs-1*.

This collection of genes, small though it is, has given a powerful boost to gerontological research and provides an important conceptual framework that future research may follow. The goal is to isolate even more longevity genes from lower animals and then to find their counterparts in the human genome. This work has already begun with the isolation of human *lag-1*. The characterization of all longevity genes is expected to revolutionize our understanding of the aging process, and it may provide the means by which the effects of age may be treated or reversed.

·7·

GERIATRICS

The World Health Organization (WHO) places health issues on a continuum from disease to impairment to disability to handicap. Geriatrics is a branch of the biomedical sciences devoted to helping the elderly (65+ years old) deal with the effects of age. The geriatric approach does not try to reverse the aging process but rather to minimize its consequences by reducing or inhibiting the progression to disability. This effort, conducted in hospitals, clinics, and nursing homes, is based on a broad range of therapies that are grounded in the biological, psychological, and social sciences.

Treating, and caring for, the elderly is a complex endeavor. Older people are usually suffering from several simultaneous disorders that, because of the patient's age, cannot be treated with the drugs or therapies that are routine for younger individuals. Drug therapies assume a clearance time (physiological deactivation of the drug), made possible by a healthy liver that may not exist in an older patient. Drugs that are safely used to treat depression or cardiovascular disease in young patients can have devastating effects on the elderly. Accurate medical histories are often difficult to obtain from elderly patients, either because of poor memory or because of psychological compensation by which the patient ignores and minimizes danger signs and symptoms. Growing old is often a time of loss: lost physical abilities, lost friends, the patient's spouse may have passed away, and the family home may have been given up for a room in a nursing home or hospital ward. All these elements complicate the diagnosis and prognosis for a geriatric patient.

The focus of this chapter is clinical geriatrics, which covers the many problems associated with the care and treatment of the elderly. We begin with the demographics of North American society with respect to age distributions, epidemiology, and the capacity of health care providers to deal with the ever-expanding geriatrics population.

Our Aging Society

Between 1900 and 1990, the total U.S. population increased threefold, while the number of elderly persons increased tenfold. In 1990 more than 35 million Americans were over the age of 65, nearly twice as many as in 1960. This number reached 35 million in 2000 (about 12 percent of the population) and is expected to increase further, to 53 million by 2020 and 75 million by 2040 (20 percent of the population). One of the fastest growing segments of the population is the very old (persons older than 85), who now account for 12 percent of all elderly persons and is expected to increase to 18 percent by 2040. In addition, the number of persons reaching 100 years of age (centenarians) is expected to increase from the current 60,000 to nearly 500,000 by 2040. In general, the mortality rate for elderly women has declined more quickly than it has for older men. In 1950 there were 89 older men for every 100 older women; in 2000 there were 70 men for every 100 women. Among the very old, there are 41 men for every 100 women. Living arrangements vary greatly for the elderly. At ages 65 to 74, one-third of women live alone, but after the age of 75, this proportion increases one-half. Before the age of 85, the elderly usually live with relatives or a spouse, but after 85, 18 percent of men and 28 percent of women live in nursing homes or hospital wards.

Per capita costs for acute and long-term (chronic) health care services are highest for the very old, so the growth of this group will have a profound effect on health care costs. Persons over 65 currently represent just over one in three of the patients seen by a primary care physician; by 2040 this ratio is expected to increase to one in two. While the costs of caring for the elderly is expected to rise, this is due not just to the patient's age but also to a general increase in the complexity and expense of diagnostic procedures and equipment. It is expected that as the proportion of older to younger persons increases, less financial and social support will be available for the elderly. Medicare and Medicaid cover much of the financial burden of caring for the elderly in the United States. However, even with these public services, the elderly still bear a considerable share of the expenses. Currently, geriatric patients can expect to pay as much as 21 percent of their income for medical care.

Evaluating the Geriatric Patient

Evaluation of a geriatric patient is much different from that of a younger individual. Young patients generally have a single complaint that the physician can focus on, and there is usually no reference to the patient's socioeconomic environment. The approach to a geriatric patient, however, may begin with the physician asking the patient to describe a typical day in his or her life. In this way, the physician can best assess the elderly person's overall quality of life, liveliness of thought, and physical independence. This approach also helps develop a good patient-physician rapport, something that is especially important to elderly patients, who often take longer to answer questions and may be shy because of it. In the initial interview, geriatricians are especially careful not to infantilize the patient by asking an attending relative questions pertaining to the patient's history or medical status. It is for this reason that geriatric patients, unless suffering from dementia, are interviewed alone. During the initial evaluation and interview, the physician attempts to gather information about the patient's medical, drug, nutrition, and psychiatric histories.

MEDICAL HISTORY   With an elderly patient, the medical history may extend back to a time when society's disease profile was different than it is today. For example, rheumatic fever and tuberculosis were much more common in the mid-1900s than they are today. Consequently, the physician will ask about diseases that were common when the patient was young. The patient will also be asked about outdated treatments, such as mercury for syphilis or pneumothorax therapy for tuberculosis. Many older persons tend to underreport symptoms out of denial or a fear of illness, disability, and the dependence these conditions may bring. Aging can also alter the individual's response to certain diseases, such as a painless myocardial infarction or pneumonia without a cough.

DRUG HISTORY   Although the physician will ask the patient, and the patient's relatives, about prescription drugs, some geriatricians have suggested that the best approach is the "brown bag" technique, whereby the patient is asked to empty his or her medicine cabinet into a brown paper bag and then to bring it to the evaluation interview. Often the complaints of older patients are traced to a drug or combination of drugs they have been taking. The drug history includes determining which drugs are used, at what dose, how often they are taken, who prescribed them, and for what reason. Topical drugs are included, such as eye drops for treating glaucoma, because there is the possibility that systemic absorption may cause unexpected side effects in the elderly. Over-the-counter drugs must be included because their overuse can have serious consequences, such as constipation from laxative use or salicylism from aspirin use. Patients are also asked to demonstrate their ability to read the labels (often printed in very small type) and to open the container, which may contain a child-resistant lid. Because older patients are often treated with multiple medications, they are at risk of noncompliance and adverse effects.

NUTRITION HISTORY   The physician tries to determine the type, quantity, and frequency of food eaten, including the number of hot meals per week. Special diets, self-prescribed fad diets, alcohol consumption, over-the-counter vitamins, and dietary fiber are also determined. For the elderly, it is very important to determine the amount of money the patient has to spend on food each week and whether suitable cooking facilities are available. The patient's ability to eat is assessed by examining the mouth and the condition of the teeth or dentures, if fitted. Poor vision, arthritis, immobility, or tremors may affect an old person's ability to prepare food. A patient that suffers from urinary incontinence may reduce fluid intake, which could also lead to poor food intake.

Managing Age-Related Disorders

The most common disorders of the elderly are dementia, cardiovascular disease, osteoporosis, and incontinence. It is not unusual for elderly patients to suffer from all these disorders simultaneously.

DEMENTIA   Nearly half of all elderly patients suffer from various degrees of dementia. Two-thirds are caused by Alzheimer's disease (AD), which is currently irreversible. Reversible dementias are caused by strokes, neoplasms, or toxins such as alcohol, or those produced by infections. Although a complete cure for most dementias is not possible, optimal management can improve the ability of these patients to cope with basic tasks. In many cases, dementia is the result of one or more small strokes caused by hypertension. Thus the first step in managing dementia is aggressive treatment for high blood pressure. This is followed with pharmacological agents that enhance cognition and function, and treat associated problems such as depression, paranoia, delusions, agitation, and even psychoses.

Where AD is suspected, the patient may be treated with cholinesterase inhibitors to maximize the half-life of brain neurotransmitters. There are three such drugs available: donepezil, rivastigmine, and galantamine. Clinical trials have shown that these drugs can improve cognitive function. However, side effects, including nausea, vomiting, and diarrhea, can lead to serious complications. Other drugs, such as estrogen (for women), vitamin E, ginkgo biloba, and nonsteroidal anti-inflammatory agents, are also used but their effectiveness is in doubt. However, while these agents may be ineffective as a treatment for advanced dementia, they may be useful in treating milder cases.

CARDIOVASCULAR DISEASE   Cardiac output and the response of the heart to exercise decreases with age. Ventricular contractions become weaker with each decade, a problem that is compounded by the age-related reduction in blood vessel elasticity. Hardening of the arteries is the prime cause of hypertension in the elderly, but it is not an unavoidable consequence of aging. The first stage in managing hypertension and cardiovascular disease is a change in lifestyle. Clinical trials have shown that even the very old can benefit by this approach, which involves maintaining an ideal body weight, no smoking, regular aerobic exercises, and a diet consisting of fruits, vegetables, and low-fat dairy products (all of which are rich in essential potassium, calcium, and magnesium). If these procedures fail to reduce blood pressure, drugs such as thiazide, beta-blockers, or calcium channel blockers may be used, but the diet and exercise regimen should be maintained.

OSTEOPOROSIS   Diminished bone mass can be determined most conveniently with special X-ray machines (dual energy X-ray absorptiometry) or with ultrasound densitometry. Both procedures determine the density as g/cm^2, which is compared to normal values from a younger population and is used to estimate the likelihood of fracture. The first attempts to manage this disease involve a diet rich in calcium and vitamin D, along with regular weight-bearing exercises. Hormone replacement therapy has also been recommended, for men and women, but as discussed in a previous chapter, this approach can lead to dangerous side effects. An alternative drug therapy involves the use of bisphosphonates, antiresorptive drugs that are known to increase bone mass. The bisphosphonate, alendronate, was shown to decrease the incidence of vertebral and nonvertebral fractures by more than 50 percent in postmenopausal women. The major side effects are gastrointestinal, and the drug must be taken on an empty stomach in an upright position.

INCONTINENCE   Incontinence, or the involuntary loss of urine or stool, is very common in the geriatric population. About 33 percent of elderly women and 20 percent of elderly men suffer from this disorder. The prevalence may be as high as 80 percent in nursing homes or long-term-care institutions. Incontinence may develop because of neurological damage sustained after a stroke or it may be traced to age-related changes in the urinary system, in particular, the integrity of the urethra and the holding volume of the bladder, which decreases with age. Delirium and exposure to a new environment, such as recent admission to hospital or nursing home, can also lead to incontinence in the elderly. Simply modifying the patient's fluid intake and eliminating diuretics such as coffee or tea can often treat transient incontinence.

Persistent or acute incontinence is managed initially by ensuring that the patient can reach a toilet quickly. It may also be necessary to provide the patient with incontinence undergarments and pads. Often with special care and training, the problem can be resolved. In other cases, it may be necessary to resort to drug therapy. A commonly used drug is a bladder relaxant, tolterodine, which is available in long-acting preparations. In severe cases, surgery may be required to repair damaged sphincters that normally regulated urine flow through the urethra.

It may also be necessary to fit the patient with a catheter that continually drains the bladder into a plastic bag. However, chronic indwelling catherization is not advised, as it is associated with a high risk of developing urinary system infections.

Drug Therapy

Geriatric patients are often prescribed a large number of drugs to deal with the many disorders they suffer from. However, as indicated above, there are usually effective nonpharmacological therapies available that should be attempted before resorting to drugs. All geriatric patients need a careful and thorough review of the drugs they are prescribed to ensure they are necessary and that there is no change of potentially dangerous drug interactions. Effective drug therapy is often hampered by faulty diagnosis. Older patients may underreport symptoms, or their complaints may be vague and multiple. In addition, symptoms of physical diseases may overlap with psychological illness. Consequently, making the correct diagnosis and prescribing the appropriate drugs is a very difficult task in geriatric medicine. Finally, the aging process alters the elderly patient's ability to deal with drugs physiologically. This deficit occurs primarily at the liver and at the kidneys.

The liver contains about 30 enzymes that are involved in the degradation of a wide variety of compounds that are consumed in an average diet. These enzymes can also handle more exotic compounds such as alcohol or pharmaceutical drugs. Age-related or even alcohol-induced deterioration of these enzymes make a safe drug dangerous when given to a geriatric patient. Potentially fatal ventricular arrhythmias have been caused by certain antihistamines when given to older patients with defective liver enzymes. However, the situation is too complex for a physician to assume that an elderly patient with normal liver function tests will be able to metabolize a given drug as efficiently as a younger patient.

The kidneys also play an important role in ridding the body of foreign or unwanted chemicals and drugs. Drugs given to older patients are cleared more slowly by the kidneys and thus have a tendency to accumulate to high, possibly toxic, levels over the time-course of treatment. Thus drugs that have not been specifically tested for use on older subjects must be used with extreme caution. Medical servicing centers and pharmaceutical companies have developed computer algorithms and databases to help evaluate drug usage and to detect possibly dangerous drug combinations that are prescribed for geriatric patients.

Nursing Homes

The poor quality of care provided in nursing homes has been known for decades. There has been some improvement since the Institute of Medicine (IOM) released a critical report in 1986, but a more recent report in 2000 indicated that serious problems still exist. One critical passage from the report indicates that "serious problems concerning quality of care apparently continue to affect residents of this country's nursing homes, and persistently poor providers of care are still in operation. Pain, pressure sores, malnutrition, and urinary incontinence have all been shown to be serious problems in recent studies of nursing home residents."

Nursing homes are intended as places where the elderly can be cared for in their final years by a team of medical professionals who specialize in geriatric medicine. In many cases, however, logistic and economic restraints make this a very difficult goal to realize. Physician involvement in nursing home care is often limited to telephone conversations with the nursing staff. Restrictive Medicare and Medicaid reimbursement policies do not encourage physicians to make more than the required monthly or 60-day visits. Physician involvement in such essential services as attendance at the medical team conferences, family meetings, and counseling residents and surrogate decision makers on treatment plans in the event of terminal illness are usually not reimbursable at all. In addition, most nursing homes lack expensive diagnostic equipment, and thus many of the residents are sent to hospital emergency rooms, where they are evaluated by staff who lack training and interest in the care of frail elderly patients.

Despite these many problems, the effectiveness of nursing homes can be improved with more attention paid to the documentation of the resident's illness and treatment history, and the introduction of nurse practitioners and physician assistants. These medical practitioners could be very helpful in implementing some of the screening and monitoring that is needed to ensure proper care of the residents, and to this extent would function as an independent patient advocate. They could also have an important role in communicating with the staff, residents, and families when the physician is not in the facility.

The problems facing nursing homes over the next 40 years are tremendous. In its report of 2000, the IOM noted the urgent need for research and data collection to obtain a better understanding and description of the various long-term-care arrangements throughout the country, including their size, the services provided, the staffing levels and training, the characteristics of those receiving care, and the staffing and quality of care provided in the different settings and services. They also called for increased funding, concluding that "the amounts and ways we pay for long-term care are probably inadequate to support a workforce sufficient in numbers, skills, stability, and commitment to provide adequate clinical and personal services for the increasingly frail or complex populations using long-term care."

Ethical Issues

The basic ethical principle governing the care of the elderly were established in the 1970s in response to allegations that human subjects in biomedical clinical trials were poorly treated. Principles of respect for persons, beneficence, and informed consent apply equally well to elderly patients in a nursing home, or hospital ward, as they do to human subjects involved in clinical trials.

RESPECT FOR PERSONS   Respect for persons, in the context of clinical trials, demands that subjects enter into research voluntarily and with adequate information. This assumes the individuals are autonomous agents, that is, are competent to make up their own minds. However, there are many instances where potential research subjects are not really autonomous; prisoners, patients in a mental institution, children, the elderly, and the infirm. All these people require special protection to ensure they are not being coerced or fooled into volunteering as research subjects. Geriatric patients are especially vulnerable because of their many medical disorders, which often affect their ability to understand what is being done to them.

BENEFICENCE   It is not enough to respect a potential subject's decisions and to protect them from harm, but in addition, it is necessary to do all that is possible to ensure their well-being. Beneficence is generally regarded as acts of kindness or charity, but in the case of geriatric patients, weakened by illness and age, it is an obligation. In this sense, it is the natural extension of the Hippocratic oath that all physicians are expected to adhere by: *I will give no deadly medicine to anyone if asked, nor suggest any such counsel.* In other words, do no harm, and for those involved in biomedical research, never injure one person to benefit another. This is particularly relevant to prescribing drugs for the elderly, who are especially sensitive to this type of therapy.

INFORMED CONSENT   All participants in clinical trials must provide informed consent in writing. Moreover, steps must be taken to ensure that the consent is, in fact, informed. This might involve an independent assessment of the individual's ability to understand the language on the consent form and any instructions or explanations the investigators have given. Geriatric patients, many of whom suffer from dementia, cannot be expected to give informed consent under many circumstances. Consequently, it is necessary to proceed with extreme caution in such cases and to ensure that an action taken, such as moving an elderly person out of their home and into an institution, is really in their best interest and not simply a convenience.

.8.

RESOURCE CENTER

Eukaryote Cell Primer

Life on Earth began 3.5 billion years ago in the form of single cells that appeared in the oceans. These cells evolved into ancestral prokaryotes and, about 2 billion years ago, gave rise to Archaea, bacteria, and eukaryotes, the three major divisions of life in the world. Eukaryotes, in turn, gave rise to plants, animals, protozoans, and fungi. Each of these groups represents a distinct phylogenetic kingdom. The Archaea and bacteria represent a fifth kingdom, known as the Monera, or prokaryotes. Archaea and bacteria are very similar anatomically, both lacking a true nucleus and internal organelles. A prokaryote genome is a single, circular piece of naked DNA, called a chromosome, containing fewer than 5,000 genes. Eukaryotes (meaning "true nucleus") are much more complex, having many membrane-bounded organelles. These include a nucleus, nucleolus, endoplasmic reticulum (ER), Golgi complex, mitochondria, lysosomes, and peroxisomes.

The eukaryote nucleus, bounded by a double phospholipid membrane, contains a DNA (deoxyribonucleic acid) genome on two or more linear chromosomes, each of which may contain up to 10,000 genes. The nucleus also contains an assembly plant for ribosomal subunits, called the nucleolus. The endoplasmic reticulum (ER) and the Golgi complex work together to glycosylate proteins and lipids (attach sugar molecules to the proteins and lipids producing glycoproteins and glycolipids), most of which are destined for the cell membrane to form a molecular "forest" known as the glycocalyx. The glycoproteins and

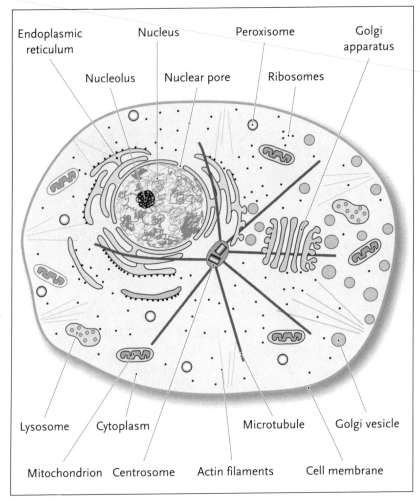

The eukaryote cell. The structural components shown here are present in organisms as diverse as protozoans, plants, and animals. The nucleus contains the DNA genome and an assembly plant for ribosomal subunits (the nucleolus). The endoplasmic reticulum (ER) and the Golgi work together to modify proteins, most of which are destined for the cell membrane. These proteins are sent to the membrane in Golgi vesicles. Mitochondria provide the cell with energy in the form of ATP. Ribosomes, some of which are attached to the ER, synthesize proteins. Lysosomes and peroxisomes recycle cellular material and molecules. The microtubules and centrosome form the spindle apparatus for moving chromosomes to the daughter cells during cell division. Actin filaments and a weblike structure consisting of intermediate filaments (not shown) form the cytoskeleton.

glycolipids travel from the ER to the Golgi, and from the Golgi to the cell surface, in membrane-bounded vesicles that form by budding off the organelle by exocytosis. Thus the cytoplasm contains many transport vesicles that originate from the ER and Golgi. The Golgi vesicles bud off the outer chamber, or the one farthest from the ER. Mitochondria, once free-living prokaryotes, and the only other organelle with a double membrane, provide the cell with energy in the form of adenosine triphosphate (ATP). The production of ATP is carried out by an assembly of metal-containing proteins, called the electron transport chain, located in the mitochondrion inner membrane. Ribosomes, some of which are attached to the ER, synthesize proteins. Lysosomes and peroxisomes recycle cellular material and molecules. The microtubules and centrosome form the spindle apparatus for moving chromosomes to the daughter cells during cell division. Actin filaments and a weblike structure consisting of intermediate filaments form the cytoskeleton.

MOLECULES OF THE CELL

Cells are biochemical entities that synthesize many thousands of molecules. Studying these chemicals, and the biochemistry of the cell, would be a daunting task were it not for the fact that most of the chemical variation is based on six types of molecules that are assembled into just four types of macromolecules. The six basic molecules are amino acids, phosphate, glycerol, sugars, fatty acids, and nucleotides. Amino acids have a simple core structure consisting of an amino group, a carboxyl group, and a variable R group attached to a carbon atom. There are 20 different kinds of amino acids, each with a unique R group. Phosphates are extremely important molecules that are used in the construction, or modification, of many other molecules. They are also used to store chemical-bond energy. Glycerol is a simple, three-carbon alcohol that is an important component of cell membranes and fat reservoirs. Sugars are extremely versatile molecules that are used as an energy source and for structural purposes. Glucose, a six-carbon sugar, is the primary energy source for most cells and it is the principle sugar used to glycosylate proteins and lipids for the production of the glycocalyx. Plants have exploited the structural potential of sugars in their production of cellulose, and thus wood, bark, grasses, and reeds are polymers of glucose and other monosaccharides. Ribose, a five-carbon sugar, is a component of nucleic acids as well as ATP. Ribose carbons are numbered as 1' (1 prime), 2', and so on. Consequently, references to nucleic acids, which include ribose, often refer to the 3' or 5' carbon. Fatty acids consist of a carboxyl group (when ionized it becomes a carboxylic acid) linked to a hydrophobic hydrocarbon tail. These molecules are used in the construction of cell membranes and fat. Nucleotides are building blocks for DNA and RNA (ribonucleic acid). Nucleotides consist of three components: a phosphate, a ribose sugar, and a nitrogenous (nitrogen containing) ring compound that behaves as a base in solution. Nucleotide bases appear in two forms: a single-ring nitrogenous base, called a pyrimidine, and a double-ringed base, called a purine. There are two kinds of purines (adenine and guanine), and three pyrimidines (uracil, cytosine, and thymine). Uracil is specific to RNA, substituting for thymine. In addition, RNA nucleotides contain ribose, whereas DNA nucleotides contain deoxyribose (hence the origin of their names). Ribose has a hydroxyl (OH) group attached to both the 2' and 3' carbons, whereas, deoxyribose is missing the 2' hydroxyl group. ATP, the molecule that is used by all cells as a source of energy, is a ribose nucleotide consisting of the purine base adenine and three phosphates attached to the 5' carbon of the ribose sugar. The phosphates are labeled α (alpha), β (beta), and γ (gamma) and are linked to the carbon in a tandem order, beginning with α. The energy stored by this molecule is carried by the covalent bonds of the β and γ phosphates. Breaking these bonds sequentially releases the energy they contain while converting ATP to adenosine diphosphate (ADP) and then to adenosine monophosphate (AMP). AMP is converted back to ATP by mitochondria.

MACROMOLECULES OF THE CELL

The six basic molecules are used by all cells to construct five essential macromolecules. These include proteins, RNA, DNA, phospholipids, and sugar polymers, known as polysaccharides. Amino acids are linked together by peptide bonds to construct a protein. A peptide bond is formed by linking the carboxyl end of one amino acid to the amino end of a second amino acid. Thus, once constructed, every protein has an amino end and a carboxyl end. An average protein may consist of 300 to 400 amino acids. Nucleic acids are macromolecules constructed from

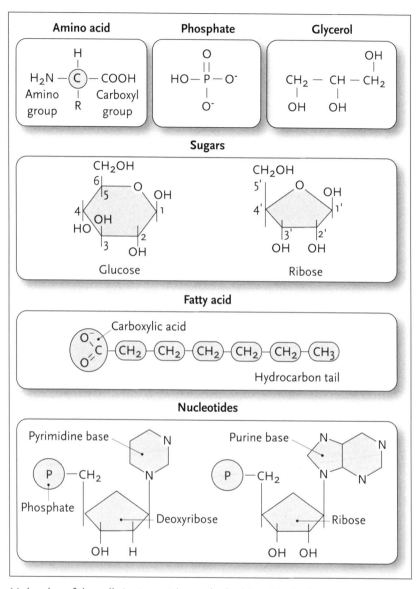

Molecules of the cell. Amino acids are the building blocks for proteins. Phosphate is an important component of many other molecules and is added to proteins to modify their behavior. Glycerol is a three-carbon alcohol that is an important ingredient in cell membranes and fat. Sugars, like glucose, are a primary energy source for most cells and also have many structural functions. Fatty acids are involved in the production of cell membranes and storage of fat. Nucleotides are the building blocks for DNA and RNA.

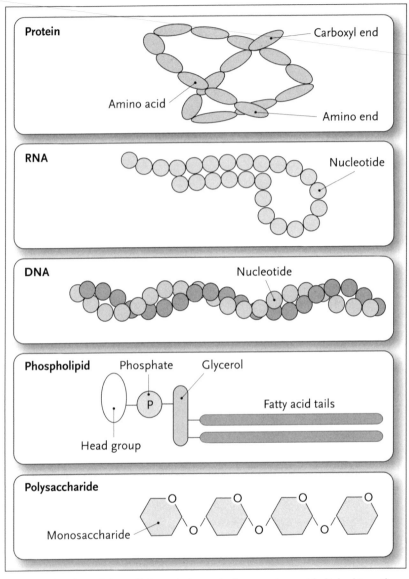

Macromolecules of the cell. Protein is made from amino acids linked together to form a long chain that can fold up into a three-dimensional structure. RNA and DNA are long chains of nucleotides. RNA is generally single stranded but can form localized double-stranded regions. DNA is a double-stranded helix, with one strand coiling around the other. A phospholipid is composed of a hydrophilic head-group, a phosphate, a glycerol molecule, and two hydrophobic fatty acid tails. Polysaccharides are sugar polymers.

nucleotides. The 5' phosphate of one nucleotide is linked to the 3' OH of a second nucleotide. Additional nucleotides are always linked to the 3' OH of the last nucleotide in the chain. Consequently, the growth of the chain is said to be in the 5' to 3' direction. RNA nucleotides are adenine, uracil, cytosine, and guanine. A typical RNA molecule consists of 2,000 to 3,000 nucleotides; it is generally single stranded but can form localized double-stranded regions. RNA is involved in the synthesis of proteins and is a structural and enzymatic component of ribosomes. DNA, a double-stranded nucleic acid, encodes cellular genes and is constructed from adenine, thymine, cytosine, and guanine deoxyribonucleotides (dATP, dTTP, dCTP, and dGTP,

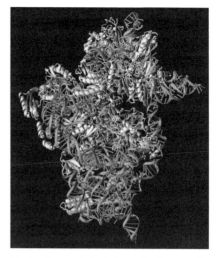

Molecule model of the 30S ribosomal subunit, which consists of protein (light gray corkscrew structures) and RNA (coiled ladders). The RNA that is also responsible for the catalytic function of the ribosome determines the overall shape of the molecule. *(Courtesy of V. Ramakrishnan, MRC Laboratory of Molecular Biology, Cambridge).*

where "d" indicates deoxyribose). The two DNA strands coil around each other like strands in a piece of rope, and for this reason the molecule is known as the double helix. DNA is an extremely large macromolecule, typically consisting of over a million nucleotide pairs (or base pairs). Double-stranded DNA forms when two chains of nucleotides interact through the formation of chemical bonds between complementary base pairs. The chemistry of the bases is such that adenine pairs with thymine, and cytosine pairs with guanine. For stability, the two strands are antiparallel, that is, the orientation of one strand is in the 5' to 3' direction, while the complementary strand runs 3' to 5'. Phospholipids, the main component of cell membranes, are composed of a polar head-group (usually an alcohol), a phosphate, glycerol, and two hydrophobic fatty acid tails. Fat that is stored in the body as an energy reserve has a structure similar to a phospholipid, being composed of three fatty acid chains attached to a molecule of glycerol. The third fatty acid takes the place of the phosphate and head-group of a phospholipid. Sugars are polymerized to form chains of two or more mono-saccharides. Disaccharides (two monosaccharides) and

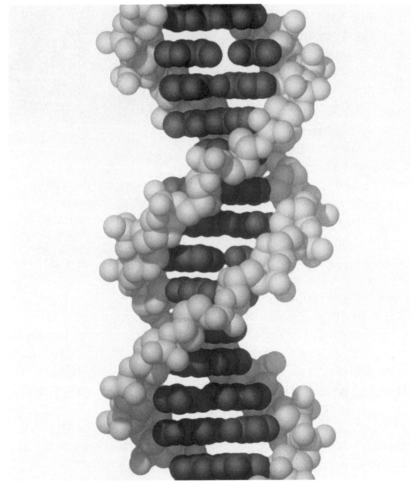

Computer model of DNA. The two strands coil around each other to form a helix that, when looking down on it from above, coils to the right. The spherical structures in this image represent the various atoms in the sugars and bases (dark gray) and phosphates (light gray). *(Kenneth Eward/BioGrafx/ Photo Researchers, Inc.)*

oligosaccharides (three to 12 monosaccharides) are attached to proteins and lipids destined for the glycocalyx. Polysaccharides, such as glycogen and starch, may contain several hundred monosaccharides and are stored in cells as an energy reserve.

THE CELL CYCLE

Cells inherited the power of reproduction from prebiotic bubbles that split in half at regular intervals under the influence of the turbulent environment that characterized the Earth more than 3 billion years ago. This pattern of turbulent fragmentation followed by a brief period of calm is now a regular behavior pattern of every cell. Even today, after 3 billion years, many cells still divide every 20 minutes.

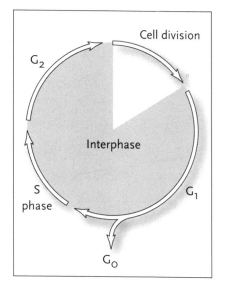

The cell cycle. Most cells spend their time cycling between a state of calm (interphase) and cell division. Interphase is further divided into three subphases: Gap 1 (G_1), S phase (DNA synthesis), and Gap 2 (G_2). Cells may exit the cycle by entering a special phase called G_0.

The regular alternation between division and calm has come to be known as the cell cycle. In studying this cycle, scientists have recognized different states of calm and different ways in which a cell can divide. The calm state of the cell cycle, referred to as interphase, is divided into three subphases, called Gap 1 (G_1), S phase (a period of DNA synthesis), and Gap 2 (G_2). The conclusion of interphase, and with it the termination of G_2, occurs with the division of the cell and a return to G_1. Cells may leave the cycle by entering a special phase called G_0. Some cells, such as postmitotic neurons in an animal's brain, remain in G_0 for the life of the organism.

Although interphase is a period of relative calm, the cell grows continuously during this period, working hard to prepare for the next round of division. Two notable events are the duplication of the spindle (the centrosome and associated microtubules), a structure that is crucial for the movement of the chromosomes during cell division, and the appearance of an enzyme called the maturation-promoting factor (MPF) at the end of G_2. MPF phosphorylates histones. The histones are proteins that bind to the DNA, which when phosphorylated, compact (or condense) the chromosomes in preparation for cell division. MPF is also responsible for the breakdown of the nuclear membrane. When cell division is complete, MPF disappears, allowing the chromosomes to decondense and the nuclear envelope to reform. Completion of a normal cell cycle always involves the division of a cell into two daughter cells. This can occur by a process known as mitosis, which is intended for cell multiplication, and by second process known as meiosis, which is intended for sexual reproduction.

MITOSIS

Mitosis is used by all free-living eukaryotes (protozoans) as a means of asexual reproduction. The growth of a plant or an animal is also accomplished with this form of cell division. Mitosis is divided into four stages: prophase, metaphase, anaphase, and telophase. All these stages are marked out in accordance with the behavior of the nucleus and the chromosomes. Prophase marks the period during which the duplicated chromosomes begin condensation, and the two centrosomes begin moving to opposite poles of the cell. Under the microscope, the chromosomes become visible as X-shaped structures, which are the two duplicated chromosomes, often called sister chromatids. A special region of each chromosome, called a centromere, holds the chromatids together. Proteins bind to the centromere to form a structure called the kinetochore (see figure, for clarity, only two chromosomes are shown). Metaphase is a period during which the chromosomes are sorted out and aligned between the two centrosomes. By this time, the nuclear membrane has completely broken down. The two centrosomes and the microtubules fanning out between them form the mitotic spindle. The area in between the spindles, where the chromosomes are aligned, is often referred to as the metaphase plate. Some of the microtubules make contact with the kinetochores, while others overlap, with motor proteins situated in between. Eukaryotes are normally diploid, so a cell

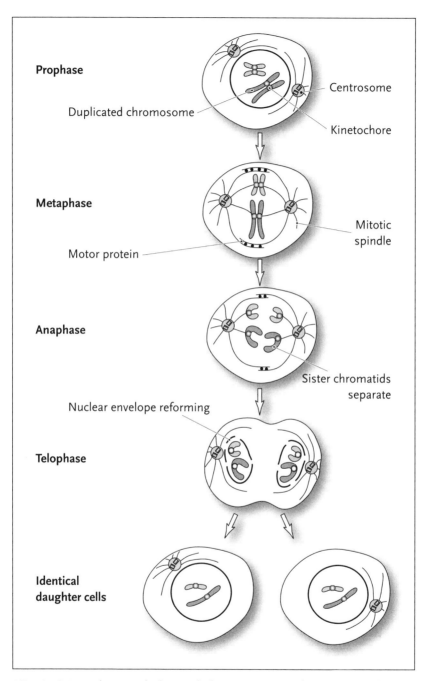

Prophase

Duplicated chromosome

Centrosome

Kinetochore

Metaphase

Motor protein

Mitotic spindle

Anaphase

Sister chromatids separate

Nuclear envelope reforming

Telophase

Identical daughter cells

Mitosis. Principal stages dealing with the movement and partitioning of the chromosomes between the future daughter cells. For clarity, only two chromosomes are shown.

would have two copies of each chromosome, one from the mother and one from the father. Anaphase is characterized by the movement of the duplicated chromosomes to opposite poles of the cell. The first step is the release of an enzyme that breaks the bonds holding the kinetochores together, thus allowing the sister chromatids to separate from each other while remaining bound to their respective microtubules. Motor proteins then move along the microtubule, dragging the chromosomes to opposite ends of the cell. Using energy supplied by ATP, the motor proteins break the microtubule down as it drags the chromosome along, so that the microtubule is gone by the time the chromosome reaches the spindle pole. Throughout this process, the motor proteins and the chromosome manage to stay one step ahead of the disintegrating microtubule. The overlapping microtubules aid movement of the chromosomes toward the poles as another type of motor protein pushes the microtubules in opposite directions, effectively forcing the centrosomes toward the poles. This accounts for the greater overlap of microtubules in metaphase as compared with anaphase. During telophase, the daughter chromosomes arrive at the spindle poles and decondense to form the relaxed chromatin characteristic of interphase nuclei. The nuclear envelope begins forming around the chromosomes, marking the end of mitosis. During the same period, a contractile ring, made of the proteins myosin and actin, begins pinching the parental cell in two. This stage, separate from mitosis, is called cytokinesis, and leads to the formation of two daughter cells, each with one nucleus.

MEIOSIS

Unlike mitosis, which leads to the growth of an organism, meiosis is intended for sexual reproduction and occurs exclusively in ovaries and testes. Eukaryotes, being diploid, receive chromosomes from both parents; if gametes were produced using mitosis, a catastrophic growth in the number of chromosomes would occur each time a sperm fertilized an egg. Meiosis is a special form of cell division that produces haploid gametes (eggs and sperm), each possessing half as many chromosomes as the diploid cell. When haploid gametes fuse, they produce an embryo with the correct number of chromosomes.

The existence of meiosis was first suggested 100 years ago, when microbiologists counted the number of chromosomes in somatic and

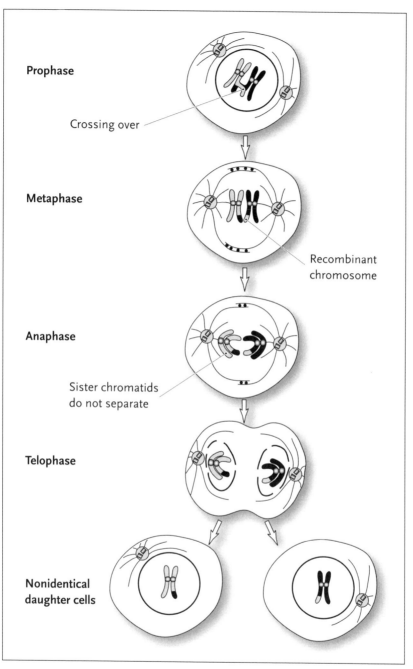

Prophase

Crossing over

Metaphase

Recombinant
chromosome

Anaphase

Sister chromatids
do not separate

Telophase

**Nonidentical
daughter cells**

Meiosis I. The most notable features include genetic recombination (crossing over) between the homologous chromosomes during prophase, comigration of the sister chromatids during anaphase, and the production of nonidentical daughter cells. Only one homologous pair is shown.

germ cells. The roundworm, for example, was found to have four chromosomes in its somatic cells but only two in its gametes. Many other studies also compared the amount of DNA in nuclei from somatic cells and gonads, always with the same result: The amount of DNA in somatic cells is exactly double the amount in fully mature gametes. To understand how this could be, scientists studied cell division in the gonads and were able to show that meiosis occurs as two rounds of cell division with only one round of DNA synthesis. The two rounds of division were called meiosis I and meiosis II, and scientists observed that both could be divided into the same four stages known to occur in mitosis. Indeed, meiosis II is virtually identical to a mitotic division. Meiosis I resembles mitosis, but close examination shows three important differences: gene swapping occurs between homologous chromosomes in prophase; homologs (i.e., two homologous chromosomes) remain paired at metaphase, instead of lining up at the plate as is done in mitosis; and the kinetochores do not separate at anaphase.

Homologous chromosomes are two identical chromosomes that come from different parents. For example, humans have 23 chromosomes from the father and the same 23 from the mother. We each have a maternal chromosome 1 and a paternal chromosome 1; they carry the same genes but specify slightly different traits. Chromosome 1 may carry the gene for eye color, but the maternal version, or allele, may specify blue eyes, whereas the paternal allele specifies brown. During prophase, homologous pairs exchange large numbers of genes by swapping whole pieces of chromosome. Thus one of the maternal chromatids (gray in the figure on page 87) ends up with a piece of paternal chromosome, and a paternal chromatid receives the corresponding piece of maternal chromosome. Mixing genetic material in this way is unique to meiosis, and it is one of the reasons sexual reproduction has been such a powerful evolutionary force.

During anaphase of meiosis I, the kinetochores do not separate as they do in mitosis. The effect of this is to separate the maternal and paternal chromosomes by sending them to different daughter cells, although the segregation is random. That is, the daughter cells receive a random assortment of maternal and paternal chromosomes, rather than one daughter cell receiving all paternal chromosomes and the other all maternal chromosomes. Random segregation, along with genetic recombination, accounts for the fact that while children resemble their parents, they do not look or act exactly like them. These two mechanisms are responsible for the remarkable adaptability of all eukaryotes. Meiosis II begins immediately after the completion of meiosis I, which produces two daughter cells each containing a duplicated parent chromosome and a recombinant chromosome consisting of both paternal and maternal DNA. These two cells divide mitotically to produce four haploid cells, each of which is genetically unique, containing unaltered or recombinant maternal and paternal chromosomes. Meiosis produces haploid cells by passing through two rounds of cell division with only one round of DNA synthesis. However, as we have seen, the process is not just concerned with reducing the number of chromosomes but is also involved in stirring up the genetic pot in order to produce unique gametes that may someday give rise to an equally unique individual.

DNA REPLICATION

DNA replication, which occurs during the S phase of the cell cycle, requires the coordinated effort of a team of enzymes, led by DNA helicase and primase. The helicase is a remarkable enzyme that is responsible for separating the two DNA strands, a feat that it accomplishes at an astonishing rate of 1,000 nucleotides every second. This enzyme gets its name from the fact that it unwinds the DNA helix as it separates the two strands. The enzyme responsible for reading the template strand, and for synthesizing the new daughter strand, is called DNA polymerase. This enzyme reads the parental DNA in the 3' to 5' direction and creates a daughter strand that grows 5' to 3'. DNA polymerase also has an editorial function; in that it checks the preceding nucleotide to make sure it is correct before it adds a nucleotide to the growing chain. The editor function of this enzyme introduces an interesting problem: How can the polymerase add the very first nucleotide when it has to check a preceding nucleotide before adding a new one? A special enzyme, called primase, which is attached to the helicase, solves this problem. Primase synthesizes short pieces of RNA that form a DNA-RNA double-stranded region. The RNA becomes a temporary part of the daughter strand, thus priming the DNA polymerase by providing the crucial first nucleotide in the new strand. Once the chromosome is duplicated,

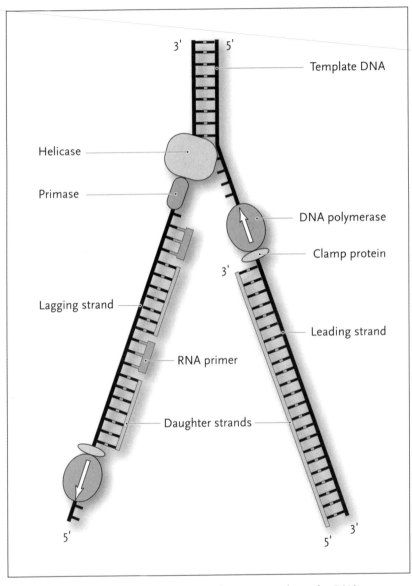

DNA replication. The helicase separates the two strands so the DNA polymerase can synthesize new strands. The primase provides replication signals for the polymerase, in the form of RNA primers, and the clamp protein keeps the polymerase from falling off the DNA. The leading strand requires only a single primer (not shown). The lagging strand requires many primers, and the daughter strand is synthesized as a series of DNA fragments that are later joined into one continuous strand.

DNA repair enzymes remove the RNA primers and replace them with DNA nucleotides.

TRANSCRIPTION, TRANSLATION, AND THE GENETIC CODE

Genes encode proteins and several kinds of RNA. Extracting the information from DNA requires the processes of transcription and translation. Transcription, catalyzed by the enzyme RNA polymerase, copies one strand of the DNA into a complementary strand of messenger RNA (mRNA) or ribosomal RNA (rRNA) that is used in the construction of ribosomes. Messenger RNA translocates to the cytoplasm, where it is translated into a protein by ribosomes. Newly transcribed rRNA is sent to the nucleolus for ribosome assembly and is never translated. Ribosomes are complex structures consisting of about 50 proteins and four kinds of rRNA, known as 5S, 5.8S, 18S, and 28S rRNA (the "S" refers to a sedimentation coefficient that is proportional to size). These RNAs range in size from about 500 bases up to 2,000 bases for the 28S. The ribosome is assembled in the nucleolus as two nonfunctional subunits before being sent out to the cytoplasm, where they combine, along with an mRNA, to form a fully functional unit. The production of ribosomes in this way ensures that translation never occurs in the nucleus.

The genetic code provides a way for the translation machinery to interpret the sequence information stored in the DNA molecule, and represented by mRNA. DNA is a linear sequence of four different kinds of nucleotides, so the simplest code could be one in which each nucleotide specifies a different amino acid. That is, adenine coding for the amino acid glycine, cytosine for lysine, and so on. The first cells may have used this coding system, but it is limited to the construction of proteins consisting of only four different kinds of amino acids. Eventually, a more elaborate code evolved in which a combination of three out of the four possible DNA nucleotides, called codons, specifies a single amino acid. With this scheme, it is possible to have a unique code for each of the 20 naturally occurring amino acids. For example, the codon AGC specifies the amino acid serine, whereas TGC specifies the amino acid cysteine. Thus a gene may be viewed as a long continuous sequence of codons. However, not all codons specify

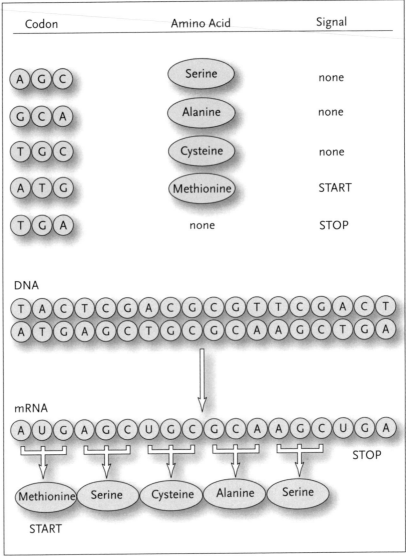

Transcription, translation, and the genetic code. Five codons are shown, four specifying amino acids (protein subunits) and two of the five serving as start and stop signals. The codons, including the start and stop signals, are linked together to form a gene on the bottom, or coding, DNA strand. The coding strand is copied into messenger RNA (mRNA), which is used to synthesize the protein. Nucleotides appear as round beads: Adenine (A), Thymine (T), Cytosine (C), and Guanine (G). Amino acids appear as labeled elliptical beads. Note that in mRNA, uracil (U) replaces the thymine (T) found in DNA.

an amino acid. The sequence TGA signals the end of the gene, and a special codon, ATG, signals the start site, in addition to specifying the amino acid methionine. Consequently, all proteins begin with this amino acid, although it is sometimes removed once construction of the protein is complete. As mentioned above, an average protein may consist of 300 to 400 amino acids; since the codon consists of three nucleotides for each amino acid, a typical gene may be 900 to 1,200 nucleotides long.

POWER GENERATION

ATP is produced in mitochondria from AMP, or ADP, and phosphate (PO_4). This process involves a number of metal-binding proteins, called the respiratory chain (also known as the electron transport chain), and a special ion channel-enzyme called ATP synthetase. The respiratory chain consists of three major components: NADH dehydrogenase, cytochrome b, and cytochrome oxidase. All these components are protein complexes that have an iron (NADH dehydrogenase, cytochrome b) or a copper core (cytochrome oxidase), and together with the ATP synthetase are located in the inner membrane of the mitochondria. The respiratory chain is analogous to an electric cable that transports electricity from a hydroelectric dam to our homes, where it is used to turn on lights or run our stereos. The human body, like that of all animals, generates electricity by processing food molecules through a metabolic pathway, called the Krebs cycle. The electricity, or electrons generated, travel through the respiratory chain, and as they do, they power the synthesis of ATP. All electric circuits must have a ground, that is, the electrons need someplace to go once they have completed the circuit. In the case of the respiratory chain, the ground is oxygen. After passing through the chain, the electrons are picked up by oxygen, which combines with hydrogen ions to form water.

THE GLYCOCALYX

This structure is an enormously diverse collection of glycoproteins and glycolipids that covers the surface of every cell, like trees on the surface of the Earth, and has many important functions. All eukaryotes originated from free-living cells that hunted bacteria for food. The glycocalyx evolved to meet the demands of this kind of lifestyle, providing a way for the cell to locate, capture, and ingest food molecules or prey organisms. Cell-surface glycoproteins also form transporters and ion channels that serve as gateways into the cell. Neurons have refined ion

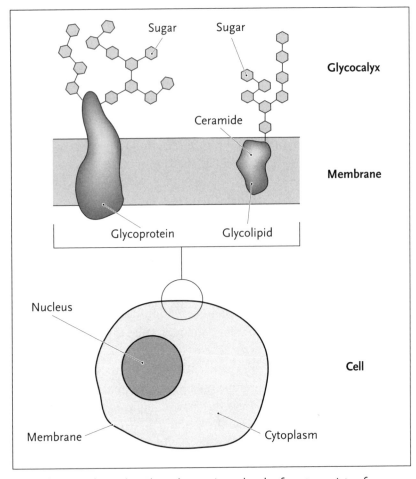

The eukaryote glycocalyx. The eukaryote's molecular forest consists of glycoproteins and glycolipids. Two examples are shown at the top: a glycoprotein on the left and a glycolipid on the right. The glycoprotein trees have "trunks" made of protein and "leaves" made of sugar molecules. Glycolipids also have "leaves" made of sugar molecules, but the "trunks" are a fatty compound called ceramide that is completely submerged within the plane of the membrane. The glycocalyx has many jobs, including cell-to-cell communication and the transport and detection of food molecules. It also provides recognition markers so the immune system can detect foreign cells.

channels for the purpose of cell-to-cell communication, giving rise to the nervous systems found in most animal species. In higher vertebrates, certain members of the glycocalyx are used by cells of the immune system as recognition markers to detect invading microbes or foreign cells introduced as an organ or tissue transplant.

Recombinant DNA Primer

Recombinant technology is a collection of procedures that makes it possible to isolate a gene and produce enough of it for a detailed study of its structure and function. Central to this technology is the ability to construct libraries of DNA fragments that represent the genetic repertoire of an entire organism or of a specific cell type. Constructing these libraries involves splicing different pieces of DNA together to form a novel or recombinant genetic entity, from which the procedure derives its name. DNA cloning and library construction were made possible by the discovery of DNA-modifying enzymes that can seal two pieces of DNA together or can cut DNA at sequence-specific sites. Many of the procedures that are part of recombinant technology, such as DNA sequencing or filter hybridization, were developed in order to characterize DNA fragments that were isolated from cells or gene libraries. Obtaining the sequence of a gene has made it possible to study the organization of the genome, but more important, it has provided a simple way of determining the protein sequence and the expression profile for any gene.

DNA-MODIFYING ENZYMES

Two of the most important enzymes used in recombinant technology are those that can modify DNA by sealing two fragments together and others that can cut DNA at specific sites. The first modifying enzyme to be discovered was DNA ligase, an enzyme that can join two pieces of DNA together and is an important component of the cell's DNA replication and repair machinery. Other DNA modifying enzymes, called restriction enzymes, cut DNA at sequence-specific sites, with different members of the family cutting at different sites. Restriction enzymes are isolated from bacteria, and since their discovery in 1970, more than 90 such enzymes have been isolated from more than 230 bacterial strains.

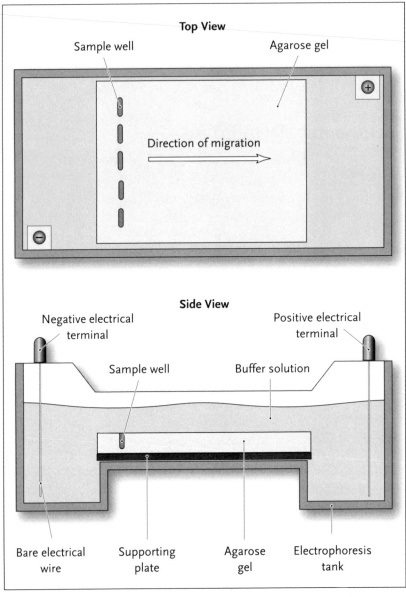

Top View

Sample well

Agarose gel

Direction of migration

Side View

Negative electrical terminal

Positive electrical terminal

Sample well

Buffer solution

Bare electrical wire

Supporting plate

Agarose gel

Electrophoresis tank

Agarose gel electrophoresis. An agarose gel is placed in an electrophoresis tank and submerged in a buffer solution. The electric terminals are connected to a power source, with the sample wells positioned near the negative terminal. When the current is turned on, the negatively charged nucleic acids migrate toward the positive terminal. The migration rate is an inverse function of molecular size. (Large molecules travel slower than small ones.)

The name "restriction enzyme" is cryptic and calls for an explanation. During the period when prokaryotes began to appear on Earth, their environment contained a wide assortment of molecules that were released into the soil or water by other cells, either deliberately or when the cells died. DNA of varying lengths was among these molecules and was readily taken up by living cells. If the foreign DNA contained complete genes from a competing bacterial species, there was the real possibility that those genes could have been transcribed and translated by the host cell with potentially fatal results. As a precaution, prokaryotes evolved a set of enzymes that would *restrict* the foreign DNA population by cutting it up into smaller pieces before being broken down completely to individual nucleotides.

GEL ELECTROPHORESIS

This procedure is used to separate different DNA and RNA fragments in a slab of agar or polyacrylamide subjected to an electric field. Nucleic acids carry a negative charge and thus will migrate toward a positively charged electrode. The gel acts as a sieving medium that impedes the movement of the molecules. Thus the rate at which the fragments migrate is a function of their size; small fragments migrate more rapidly than large fragments. The gel, containing the samples, is run submerged in a special pH-regulated solution, or buffer, containing a nucleic-acid-specific dye, ethidium bromide. This dye produces a strong reddish-yellow fluorescence when exposed to ultraviolet (UV) radiation. Consequently, after electrophoresis, the nucleic acid can be detected by photographing the gel under UV illumination.

DNA CLONING

In 1973 scientists discovered that restriction enzymes, DNA ligase, and bacterial plasmids could be used to clone DNA molecules. Plasmids are small (about 4,000 base pairs, also expressed as 4.0 kilo base pairs or 4 Kbp) circular minichromosomes that occur naturally in bacteria and are often exchanged between cells by passive diffusion. When a bacterium acquires a new plasmid, it is said to have been transfected. For bacteria, the main advantage to swapping plasmids is that they often carry antibiotic resistance genes, so that a cell sensitive to ampicillin can become resistant simply by acquiring the right plasmid.

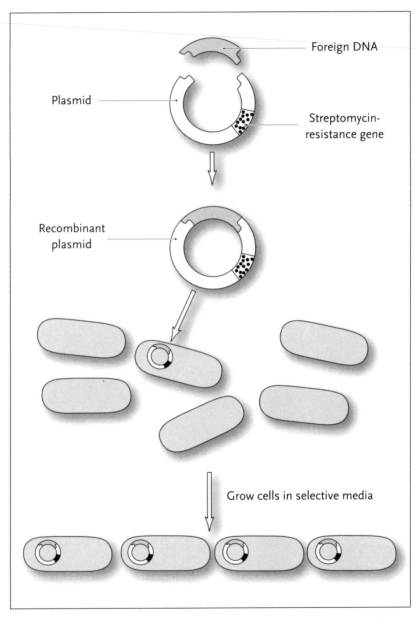

Cloning DNA in a plasmid. The foreign DNA and the plasmid are cut with the same restriction enzyme, allowed to fuse, and then sealed with DNA ligase. The recombinant plasmid is mixed with bacterial cells, some of which pick up the plasmid, allowing them to grow in a culture medium containing the antibiotic streptomycin. The bacteria's main chromosome is not shown.

The first cloning experiment used a plasmid from *Escherichia coli* that was cut with the restriction enzyme *Eco*RI. The plasmid had a single *Eco*RI site, so the restriction enzyme simply opened the circular molecule, rather than cutting it up into many useless pieces. Foreign DNA, cut with the same restriction enzyme, was incubated with the plasmid. Because the plasmid and foreign DNA were both cut with *Eco*RI, the DNA could insert itself into the plasmid to form a hybrid, or recombinant plasmid, after which DNA ligase sealed the two together. The reaction mixture was added to a small volume of *E. coli* so that some of the cells could take up the recombinant plasmid before being transferred to a nutrient broth containing streptomycin. Only those cells carrying the recombinant plasmid, which contained an antistreptomycin gene, could grow in the presence of this antibiotic. Each time the cells divided, the plasmid DNA was duplicated along with the main chromosome. After the cells had grown overnight, the foreign DNA had been amplified, or cloned, billions of times and was easily isolated for sequencing or expression studies.

GENOMIC AND cDNA LIBRARIES

The basic cloning procedure described above not only provides a way to amplify a specific piece of DNA, but it can also be used to construct gene libraries. In this case, however, the cloning vector is a bacteriophage, called lambda. The lambda genome is double-stranded linear DNA of about 40 Kbp, much of which can be replaced by foreign DNA without sacrificing the ability of the virus to infect bacteria. This is the great advantage of lambda over a plasmid. Lambda can accommodate very long pieces of DNA, often long enough to contain an entire gene, whereas a plasmid cannot accommodate foreign DNA that is larger than four Kbp. Moreover, bacteriophage has the natural ability to infect bacteria, so the efficiency of transfection is 100 times greater than it is for plasmids.

The construction of a gene library begins by isolating genomic DNA and digesting it with a restriction enzyme to produce fragments of 1,000 to 10,000 base pairs. These fragments are ligated into lambda genomes, which are subjected to a packaging reaction to produce mature viral particles, most of which carry a different piece of the genomic DNA. This collection of viruses is called a genomic library and is used to study the structure and organization of specific genes. Clones from a library such as this contains the coding sequences, in addition to introns, intervening sequences, promoters, and enhancers. An alternative form of a gene library can be constructed by isolating mRNA from a specific cell type. This RNA is converted to the complementary DNA (cDNA) using an RNA-dependent DNA polymerase called reverse transcriptase. The cDNA is ligated to lambda genomes and packaged for the genomic library. This collection of recombinant viruses is a cDNA library and only contains genes that were being expressed by the cells when the RNA was extracted. It does not include introns or controlling elements, as these are lost during transcription and the processing that occurs in the cell to make mature mRNA. Thus a cDNA library is intended for the purpose of studying gene expression and the structure of the coding region only.

LABELING CLONED DNA

Many of the procedures used in the area of recombinant technology were inspired by the events that occur during DNA replication. This includes the labeling of cloned DNA for use as probes in expression studies, DNA sequencing, and polymerase chain reaction (PCR, described in a following section). DNA replication involves duplicating one of the strands (the parent or template strand) by linking nucleotides in an order specified by the template and depends on a large number of enzymes, the most important of which is DNA polymerase. This enzyme, guided by the template strand, constructs a daughter strand by linking nucleotides together. One such nucleotide is deoxyadenine triphosphate (dATP). Deoxyribonucleotides have a single hydroxyl group located at the 3' carbon of the sugar group, while the triphosphate is attached to the 5' carbon. The procedure for labeling DNA probes, developed in 1983, introduces radioactive nucleotides into a DNA molecule. This method supplies DNA polymerase with a single-stranded DNA template, a primer, and the four nucleotides in a buffered solution to induce *in vitro* replication. The daughter strand, which becomes the probe, is labeled by including a nucleotide in the reaction mix that is linked to a radioactive isotope. The radioactive nucleotide is usually deoxycytosine triphosphate (dCTP) or dATP.

Single-stranded DNA hexamers (six bases long) are used as primers, and these are produced in such a way that they contain all possible permutations of four bases taken six at a time. Randomizing the base sequence for the primers ensures there will be at least one primer site in a template that is only 50 bp long. Templates used in labeling reactions such as this are generally 100 to 800 bp long. This strategy of labeling DNA, known as random primer or oligo labeling, is widely used in cloning and in DNA and RNA filter hybridizations (described in the following sections).

DNA SEQUENCING

A sequencing reaction developed by the British biochemist Dr. Fred Sanger in 1976 is another technique that takes its inspiration from the natural process of DNA replication. DNA polymerase requires a primer with a free 3' hydroxyl group. The polymerase adds the first nucleotide to this group, and all subsequent bases are added to the 3' hydroxyl of the previous base. Sequencing by the Sanger method is usually

EXAMPLE OF A SEQUENCING REACTION		
Tube	**Reaction Products**	
A	G-C-A-T-C-G-T-C C-G-T-**A**	G-C-A-T-C-G-T-C C-G-T-A-G-C-**A**
T	G-C-A-T-C-G-T-C C-G-**T**	
C	G-C-A-T-C-G-T-C **C**	G-C-A-T-C-G-T-C C-G-T-A-G-**C**
G	G-C-A-T-C-G-T-C C-**G**	G-C-A-T-C-G-T-C C-G-T-A-**G**
	G-C-A-T-C-G-T-C C-G-T-A-G-C-A-**G**	

The Sanger sequencing reaction is set up in four separate tubes, each containing a different dideoxynucleotide (ddATP, ddTTP, ddCTP, and ddGTP). The reaction products are shown for each of the tubes: A (ddATP), T (ddTTP), C (ddCTP), and G (ddGTP). The template strand is GCATCGTC. Replication of the template begins after the primer binds to the primer site on the sequencing plasmid. The dideoxynucleotide terminating the reaction is shown in bold. The daughter strands, all of different lengths, are fractionated on a polyacrylamide gel.

performed with the DNA cloned into a plasmid. This simplifies the choice of the initial primers because their sequence can be derived from the known plasmid sequence. An engineered plasmid primer site adjacent to a cloned DNA fragment is shown in the figure. Once the primer binds to the primer site, the cloned DNA may be replicated. Sanger's innovation involved the synthesis of artificial nucleotides lacking the 3' hydroxyl group, thus producing dideoxynucleotides (ddATP, ddCTP, ddGTP, and ddTTP). Incorporation of a dideoxynucleotide terminates the growth of the daughter strand at that point, and this can be used to determine the size of each daughter strand. The shortest daughter strand represents the complementary nucleotide at the beginning of the template, whereas the longest strand represents the complementary nucleotide at the end of the template (see table). The reaction products, consisting of all the daughter strands are fractionated on a polyactylamide gel. Polyacrylamide serves the same function as agarose. It has the advantage of being a tougher material, essential for the large size of a typical sequencing gel. Some of the nucleotides included in the Sanger reaction are labeled with a radioactive isotope so the fractionated daughter strands can be visualized by drying the gel and then exposing it to X-ray film. Thus the Sanger method uses the natural process of replication to mark the position of each nucleotide in the DNA fragment so the sequence of the fragment can be determined.

A representation of a sequencing gel is shown in the accom-

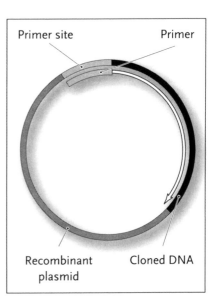

Plasmid primer site for DNA sequencing. The cloned DNA is inserted into the plasmid near an engineered primer site. Once the primer binds to the primer site, the cloned DNA may be replicated, as part of a sequencing reaction, in the direction indicated by the arrow. Only one strand of the double-stranded plasmid, and cloned DNA, is shown.

panying figure. The sequence of the daughter strand is read beginning with the smallest fragment at the bottom of the gel and ending with the largest fragment at the top. The sequence of the template strand (see table on page 101) is obtained simply by taking the complement of the sequence obtained from the gel (the daughter strand).

SOUTHERN AND NORTHERN BLOTTING

One of the most important techniques to be developed, as part of recombinant technology, is the transfer of nucleic acids from an agarose gel to nylon filter paper that can be hybridized to a labeled probe to detect specific genes. This procedure was introduced by the Scottish scientist E. M. Southern in 1975 for transferring DNA and is now known as Southern blotting. Since the DNA is transferred to filter paper, the detection stage is known as

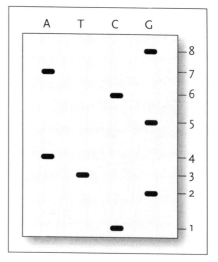

A representation of a sequencing gel. The reaction products run from the top to the bottom, with the smallest fragment migrating at the highest rate. The sequence is read beginning with the smallest fragment on the gel (band #1, in the "C" lane) and ending with the largest fragment at the top (band #8, in the "G" lane). The sequence is CGTAGCAG. The complementary sequence is GCATCGTC. This is the template strand indicated in the table on page 101.

filter hybridization. In 1980 the procedure was modified to transfer RNA to nylon membranes for the study of gene expression and, in reference to the original, is called northern blotting.

Northern blotting is used to study the expression of specific genes and is usually performed on messenger RNA (mRNA). Typical experiments may wish to determine the expression of specific genes in normal, as opposed to cancerous, tissue or tissues obtained from groups of different ages. The RNA is fractionated on an agarose gel and then transferred to a nylon membrane. The paper towels placed on top of the assembly pull the transfer buffer through the gel, eluting the RNA from the gel and trapping it on the membrane. The location of specific mRNA can be determined by hybridizing the membrane to a radiolabeled cDNA or genomic clone. The hybridization procedure involves placing the filter in a buffer solution containing a labeled probe. During a long incubation period, the probe binds to the target sequence immobilized on the membrane. A-T and G-C base pairing mediate the binding between the probe and target. The double-stranded molecule that is formed is a hybrid, being formed between the RNA target on the membrane and the DNA probe.

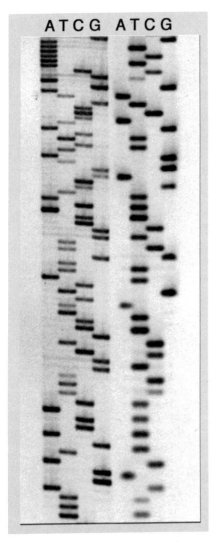

An autoradiogram of a portion of a DNA sequencing gel. A partial sequence (the first 20 bases) of the left set, beginning at the bottom of the "T" lane, is TTTAGGATGACCACTTTGGC. (Dr. Joseph Panno)

FLUORESCENT IN SITU HYBRIDIZATION (FISH)

Studying gene expression does not always depend on northern blots and filter hybridization. In the 1980s, scientists found that cDNA probes could be hybridized to DNA or mRNA in situ, that is, while located within cells or tissue sections fixed on microscope slide. In this case, the probe is labeled with a fluorescent dye molecule, rather than a radioactive isotope. The samples are then examined and photographed under a fluorescent microscope. FISH is an extremely

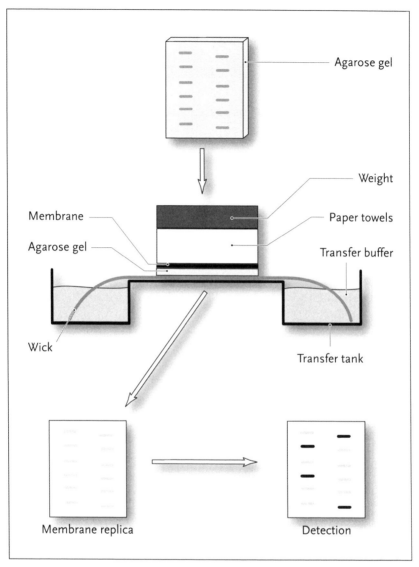

Northern transfer and membrane hybridization. RNA is fractionated on an agarose gel and then placed face down on a paper wick in a transfer tank. The gel is overlain with a piece of nylon membrane, paper towels, and weight. The paper towels draw the buffer through the gel and the membrane. The flow of buffer elutes the RNA from the gel, transferring it to the membrane. A radiolabeled cDNA probe is hybridized to the membrane to detect specific mRNA transcripts. Note that the thickness of the membrane is exaggerated for clarity.

powerful variation on Southern and northern blots. This procedure gives precise information regarding the identity of a cell that expresses a specific gene, information that usually cannot be obtained with filter hybridization. Organs and tissues are generally composed of many different kinds of cells that cannot be separated from each other using standard biochemical extraction procedures. Histological sections, however, show clearly the various cell types and, when subjected to FISH analysis, provide clear results as to which cells express specific genes. FISH is also used in clinical laboratories for the diagnosis of genetic abnormalities.

POLYMERASE CHAIN REACTION (PCR)

PCR is simply repetitive DNA replication over a limited, primer-defined region of a suitable template. The region defined by the primers is amplified to such an extent that it can be easily isolated for further study. The reaction exploits the fact that a DNA duplex in a low-salt buffer will melt (i.e., separate into two single strands) at 75°C, but will re-anneal (rehybridize) at 37°C. The reaction is initiated by melting the template in the presence of primers and polymerase in a suitable buffer, cooling quickly to 37°C, and allowing sufficient time for the polymerase to replicate both strands of the template. The temperature is then increased to 75°C to melt the newly formed duplexes and then cooled to 37°C. At the lower temperature, more primer will anneal to initiate another round of replication. The heating-cooling cycle is repeated 20 to 30 times, after which the reaction products are fractionated on an agarose gel and photographed. The band containing the amplified fragment may be cut out of the gel and purified for further study. The DNA polymerase used in these reactions is isolated from thermophilic bacteria that can withstand temperatures of 70°C to 80°C. PCR applications are nearly limitless. It is used to amplify DNA from samples containing, at times, no more than a few cells. It can be used to screen libraries and to identify genes that are turned on or off during embryonic development or during cellular transformation.

Gene Therapy Primer

When we get sick, it often is due to invading microbes that destroy or damage cells and organs in our body. Cholera, smallpox, measles, diphtheria, AIDS, and the common cold are all examples of what we call an infectious disease. If we catch any of these diseases, our doctor may prescribe a drug that will, in some cases, remove the microbe from our bodies, thus curing the disease. Unfortunately, most of the diseases we fall prey to are not of the infectious kind. In such cases, there are no microbes to fight, no drugs to apply. Instead, we are faced with a far more difficult problem, for this type of disease is an ailment that damages a gene. Gene therapy attempts to cure these diseases by replacing or supplementing the damaged gene.

When a gene is damaged, it usually is caused by a point mutation, a change that affects a single nucleotide. Sickle-cell anemia, a disease affecting red blood cells, was the first genetic disorder of this kind to be described. The mutation occurs in a gene that codes for the β (beta) chain of hemoglobin, converting the codon GAG to GTG, which substitutes the amino acid valine at position 6 for glutamic acid. This single amino-acid substitution is enough to cripple the hemoglobin molecule, making it impossible for it to carry enough oxygen to meet the demands of a normal adult. Scientists have identified several thousand genetic disorders that are known to be responsible for diseases such as breast cancer, colon cancer, hemophilia, and two neurological disorders, Alzheimer's disease and Parkinson's disease.

Gene therapy is made possible by recombinant DNA technology (biotechnology). Central to this technology is the use of viruses to clone specific pieces of DNA. That is, the DNA is inserted into a viral chromosome and is amplified as the virus multiplies. Viruses are parasites that specialize in infecting bacterial and animal cells. Consequently, scientists realized that a therapeutic gene could be inserted into a patient's cells by first introducing it into a virus and then letting the virus carry it into the affected cells. In this context the virus is referred to as a gene therapy delivery vehicle or vector (in recombinant technology, it is referred to as a cloning vector).

Commonly used viruses are the retrovirus and the adenovirus. A retrovirus gets its name from the fact that it has an RNA genome that is copied into DNA after it infects a cell. Corona viruses (which cause the common cold) and the AIDS virus are common examples of retroviruses. The adenovirus (from "adenoid," a gland from which the virus was first isolated) normally infects the upper respiratory tract, causing colds and flulike symptoms. This virus, unlike the retrovirus, has a DNA genome. Artificial vectors, called liposomes, have also been used that consist of a phospholipid vesicle (bubble) containing the therapeutic gene.

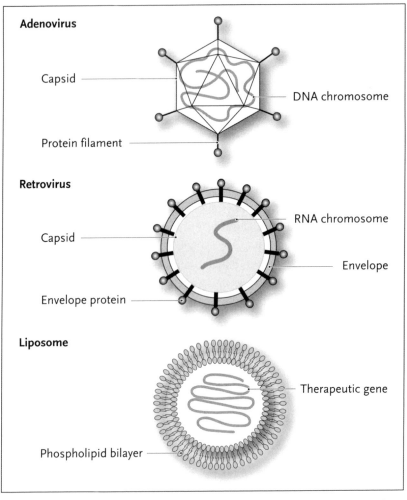

Vectors used in gene therapy. Adenoviruses have a DNA genome contained in a crystalline protein capsid, and normally infect cells of the upper respiratory tract, causing colds and flulike symptoms. The protein filaments are used to infect cells. Retroviruses have an RNA genome that is converted to DNA when a cell is infected. The capsid is enclosed in a phospholipid envelope, studded with proteins that are used to infect cells. The HIV (AIDS) virus is a common example of a retrovirus. Artificial vectors have also been used, consisting of a phospholipid bilayer enclosing the therapeutic gene.

Vector preparation and delivery. A viral chromosome and a therapeutic gene are cut with the same restriction enzyme and joined together, after which the recombinant chromosome is packaged into viral particles to form the vector. The vector may be introduced into cultured cells and then returned to the patient from whom they were derived (*ex vivo* delivery), or the vector may be injected directly into the patient's circulatory system (*in vivo* delivery).

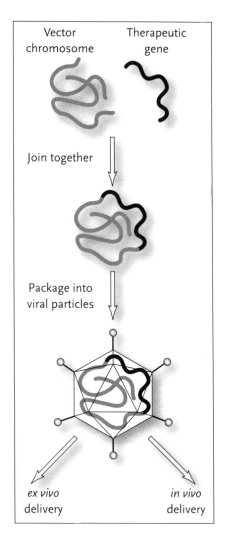

Gene therapy vectors are prepared by cutting the viral chromosome and the therapeutic gene with the same restriction enzyme, after which the two are joined together with a DNA ligase. This recombinant chromosome is packaged into viral particles to form the final vector. The vector may be introduced into cultured cells suffering from a genetic defect and then returned to the patient from whom they were derived (ex vivo delivery). Alternatively, the vector may be injected directly into the patient's circulatory system (in vivo delivery). The ex vivo procedure is used when the genetic defect appears in white blood cells, or stem cells that may be harvested from the patient and grown in culture. The in vivo procedure is used when the genetic defect appears in an organ, such as the liver, brain, or pancreas. This is the most common form of gene therapy, but it is also potentially hazardous, because vector, being free in the circulatory system, may infect a wide range of cells, thus activating an immune response that could lead to widespread tissue and organ damage.

The first gene therapy trial, conducted in 1990, used ex vivo delivery. This trail cured a young patient named Ashi deSilva of an immune deficiency (adenosine deaminase deficiency) that affects white blood cells. Other trials since then have either been ineffective or were devastating failures. Such a case occurred in 1999, when Jesse Gelsinger, an 18-year-old patient suffering from a liver disease, died while participating in a gene therapy trial. His death was caused by multiorgan failure brought on by the viral vector. In 2002, two children being treated for another form of immune deficiency developed vector-induced leukemia (cancer of the white blood cells). Despite these setbacks, gene therapy holds great promise as a medical therapy, and there are currently more than 600 trails in progress, in the United States alone, to treat a variety of genetic disorders.

The Human Genome Project

Sequencing the entire human genome is an idea that grew over a period of 20 years, beginning in the early 1980s. At that time, the DNA-sequencing method invented by the British biochemist Fred Sanger, then at the University of Cambridge, was but a few years old and had only been used to sequence viral or mitochondrial genomes (see chapter 8 for a description of sequencing methods). Indeed, one of the first genomes to be sequenced was that of bacteriophage G4, a virus that infects the bacterium *Escherichia coli (E. coli)*. The G4 genome consists of 5,577 nucleotide pairs (or base pairs, abbreviated bp) and was sequenced in Dr. Sanger's laboratory in 1979. By 1982 the Sanger protocol was used by others to sequence the genome of the animal virus SV40 (5,224 bp), the human mitochondrion (16,569 bp), and bacteriophage lambda (48,502 bp). Besides providing invaluable data, these projects demonstrated the feasibility of sequencing very large genomes.

The possibility of sequencing the entire human genome was first discussed at scientific meetings organized by the United States Department of Energy (DOE) between 1984 and 1986. A committee appointed by the U.S. National Research Council endorsed the idea in 1988 but recommended a broader program that would include the sequencing of the genes of humans, bacteria, yeast, worms, flies, and mice. They also called for the establishment of research programs devoted to the ethical, legal, and social issues raised by human genome research. The program was formally launched in late 1990 as a consortium consisting of coordinated sequencing projects in the United States, Britain, France, Germany, Japan, and China. At about the same time, the Human Genome Organization (HUGO) was founded to provide a forum for international coordination of genomic research.

By 1995 the consortium had established a strategy, called hierarchical shotgun sequencing, which they applied to the human genome as well as to the other organisms mentioned. With this strategy, genomic DNA is cut into one-megabase (Mb) fragments (i.e., each fragment consists of 1 million bases) that are cloned into bacterial artificial chromosomes (BACs) to form a library of DNA fragments. The BAC fragments are partially characterized, then organized into an overlapping assembly called a contig. Clones are selected from the contigs for shotgun sequencing. That is, each shotgun clone is digested into small 1,000 bp fragments, sequenced, and then assembled into the final sequence with the aid of computers. Organizing the initial BAC fragments into contigs greatly simplifies the final assembly stage.

Sequencing of the human genome was divided into two stages. The first stage, completed in 2001, was a rough draft that covered about 80 percent of the genome with an estimated size of more than 3 billion bases (also expressed as three gigabases, or three Gb). The final draft, completed in April 2003, covers the entire genome and refines the data for areas of the genome that were difficult to sequence. It also filled in many gaps that occurred in the rough draft. The final draft of the human genome gives us a great deal of information that may be divided into three categories: gene content, gene origins, and gene organization.

GENE CONTENT

Analysis of the final draft has shown that the human genome consists of 3.2 Gb of DNA that encodes about 30,000 genes (estimates range between 25,000 to 32,000). The estimated number of genes is surprisingly low; many scientists had believed the human genome contained

100,000 genes. By comparison, the fruit fly has 13,338 genes and the simple roundworm, *Caenorhabditis elegans (C. elegans)*, has 18,266. The genome data suggests that human complexity, as compared with the fruit fly or the worm, is not simply due to the absolute number of genes but involves the complexity of the proteins that are encoded by those genes. In general, human proteins tend to be much more complex than those of lower organisms. Data from the final draft and other sources provides a detailed overview of the functional profile of human cellular proteins.

GENE ORIGINS

Fully one-half of human genes originated as transposable elements, also known as jumping genes. Equally surprising is the fact that 220 of our genes were obtained by horizontal transfer from bacteria, rather than ancestral, or vertical, inheritance. In other words, we obtained these genes directly from bacteria, probably during episodes of infection, in a kind of natural gene therapy, or gene swapping. We know this to be the case because, while these genes occur in bacteria, they are not present in yeast, fruit flies, or any other eukaryotes that have been tested.

The function of most of the horizontally transferred genes is unclear, although a few may code for basic metabolic enzymes. A notable exception is a gene that codes for an enzyme called monoamine oxidase (MAO). Monoamines are neurotransmitters, such as dopamine, norepinephrine, and serotonin, which are needed for neural signaling in the human central nervous system. Monoamine oxidase plays a crucial role in the turnover of these neurotransmitters. How MAO, obtained from bacteria, could have developed such an important role in human physiology is a great mystery.

GENE ORGANIZATION

In prokaryotes, genes are simply arranged in tandem along the chromosome, with little if any DNA separating one gene from the other. Each gene is transcribed into messenger RNA (mRNA), which is translated into protein. Indeed, in prokaryotes, which have no nucleus, translation often begins even before transcription is complete. In eukaryotes, as we might expect, gene organization is more complex. Data from the genome project shows clearly that eukaryote genes are split into subunits, called exons, and that each exon is separated by a length of DNA, called an intron. A gene, consisting of introns and exons, is separated from other genes by long stretches of noncoding DNA called intervening sequences. Eukaryote genes are transcribed into a primary RNA molecule that includes exon and intron sequences. The primary transcript never leaves the nucleus and is never translated into protein. Nuclear enzymes remove the introns from the primary transcript, after which the exons are joined together to form the mature mRNA. Thus only the exons carry the necessary code to produce a protein.

GLOSSARY

acetyl   A chemical group derived from acetic acid. Important in energy metabolism and for the modification of proteins.

acetylcholine   A neurotransmitter released at axonal terminals by cholinergic neurons. Found in the central and peripheral nervous system and released at the vertebrate neuromuscular junction.

acetyl CoA   A water-soluble molecule, coenzyme A (CoA), that carries acetyl groups in cells.

acid   A substance that releases protons when dissolved in water. Carries a net negative charge.

actin filament   A protein filament formed by the polymerization of globular actin molecules. Forms the cytoskeleton of all eukaryotes and part of the contractile apparatus of skeletal muscle.

action potential   A self-propagating electrical impulse that occurs in the membranes of neurons, muscles, photoreceptors, and hair cells of the inner ear.

active transport   Movement of molecules across the cell membrane, utilizing the energy stored in ATP.

adenylate cyclase   A membrane-bound enzyme that catalyzes the conversion of ATP to cyclic AMP. An important component of cell-signaling pathways.

adherens junction   A cell junction in which the cytoplasmic face of the membrane is attached to actin filaments.

adipocyte   A fat cell.

adrenaline (epinephrine)   A hormone released by chromaffin cells in the adrenal gland. Prepares an animal for extreme activity, increases the heart rate and blood-sugar levels.

adult stem cells   Stem cells isolated from adult tissues, such as bone marrow or epithelium.

aerobic   Refers to a process that either requires oxygen or occurs in its presence.

allele   An alternate form of a gene. Diploid organisms have two alleles for each gene, located at the same locus (position) on homologous chromosomes.

allogeneic transplant   A patient receives a tissue or organ transplant from an unrelated individual.

alpha helix   A common folding pattern of proteins in which a linear sequence of amino acids twists into a right-handed helix stabilized by hydrogen bonds.

amino acid   An organic molecule containing amino and carboxyl groups that is a building block of protein.

aminoacyl-tRNA   An amino acid linked by its carboxyl group to a hydroxyl group on tRNA.

aminoacyl-tRNA synthetase   An enzyme that attaches the correct amino acid to a tRNA.

amino terminus   The end of a protein or polypeptide chain that carries a free amino group.

amphipathic   Having both hydrophilic and hydrophobic regions, as in a phospholipid.

anabolism   A collection of metabolic reactions in a cell whereby large molecules are made from smaller ones.

anaerobic   A cellular metabolism that does not depend on molecular oxygen.

anaphase   A mitotic stage in which the two sets of chromosomes move away from each other toward opposite spindle poles.

anchoring junction   A cell junction that attaches cells to each other.

angiogenesis   Sprouting of new blood vessels from preexisting ones.

angstrom   A unit of length, equal to 10^{-10} meter or 0.1 nanometer (nm), that is used to measure molecules and atoms.

anterior   A position close to or at the head end of the body.

antibiotic   A substance made by bacteria, fungi, and plants that is toxic to microorganisms. Common examples are penicillin and streptomycin.

antibody   A protein made by B cells of the immune system in response to invading microbes.

anticodon   A sequence of three nucleotides in tRNA that is complementary to a messenger RNA codon.

antigen   A molecule that stimulates an immune response, leading to the formation of antibodies.

antigen-presenting cell   A cell of the immune system, such as a monocyte, that presents pieces of an invading microbe (the antigen) to lymphocytes.

antiparallel   The relative orientation of the two strands in a DNA double helix; the polarity of one strand is oriented in the opposite direction to the other.

antiporter   A membrane carrier protein that transports two different molecules across a membrane in opposite directions.

apoptosis   Regulated or programmed form of cell death that may be activated by the cell itself or by the immune system to force cells to commit suicide when they become infected with a virus.

asexual reproduction   The process of forming new individuals without gametes or the fertilization of an egg by a sperm. Individuals produced this way are identical to the parent and referred to as a clone.

aster   The star-shaped arrangement of microtubules that is characteristic of a mitotic or meiotic spindle.

ATP (adenosine triphosphate)   A nucleoside consisting of adenine, ribose, and three phosphate groups that is the main carrier of chemical energy in the cell.

ATPase   Any enzyme that catalyzes a biochemical reaction by extracting the necessary energy from ATP.

ATP synthase   A protein located in the inner membrane of the mitochondrion that catalyzes the formation of ATP from ADP and inorganic phosphate using the energy supplied by the electron transport chain.

autogeneic transplant   A patient receives a transplant of his or her own tissue.

autosome   Any chromosome other than a sex chromosome.

axon   A long extension of a neuron's cell body that transmits an electrical signal to other neurons.

axonal transport   The transport of organelles, such as Golgi vesicles, along an axon to the axonal terminus. Transport also flows from the terminus to the cell body.

bacteria   One of the most ancient forms of cellular life (the other is the archaea). Bacteria are prokaryotes and some are known to cause disease.

bacterial artificial chromosome (BAC)   A cloning vector that accommodates DNA inserts of up to 1 million base pairs.

bacteriophage   A virus that infects bacteria. Bacteriophages were used to prove that DNA is the cell's genetic material and are now used as cloning vectors.

base   A substance that can accept a proton in solution. The purines and pyrimidines in DNA and RNA are organic bases and are often referred to simply as bases.

base pair   Two nucleotides in RNA or DNA that are held together by hydrogen bonds. Adenine bound to thymine or guanine bound to cytosine are examples of base pairs.

B cell (B lymphocyte)   A white blood cell that makes antibodies and is part of the adaptive immune response.

benign   Tumors that grow to a limited size and do not spread to other parts of the body.

beta sheet   Common structural motif in proteins in which different strands of the protein run alongside each other and are held together by hydrogen bonds.

biopsy   The removal of cells or tissues for examination under a microscope. When only a sample of tissue is removed, the procedure is called an incisional biopsy or core biopsy. When an entire lump or suspicious area is removed, the procedure is called an excisional biopsy. When a sample of tissue or fluid is removed with a needle, the procedure is called a needle biopsy or fine-needle aspiration.

biosphere   The world of living organisms.

bivalent   A duplicated chromosome paired with its homologous duplicated chromosome at the beginning of meiosis.

blastomere   A cell formed by the cleavage of a fertilized egg. Blastomeres are the totipotent cells of the early embryo.

blotting   A technique for transferring DNA (Southern blotting), RNA (northern blotting), or proteins (western blotting) from an agarose or polyacrylamide gel to a nylon membrane.

BRCA1 (breast cancer gene 1)   A gene on chromosome 17 that may be involved in regulating the cell cycle. A person who inherits an altered version of the BRCA1 gene has a higher risk of getting breast, ovarian, or prostate cancer.

BRCA2 (breast cancer gene 2) A gene on chromosome 13 that, when mutated, increases the risk of getting breast, ovarian, or prostate cancer.

budding yeast The common name for the baker's yeast *Saccharomyces cerevisiae*, a popular experimental organism that reproduces by budding off a parental cell.

cadherin Belongs to a family of proteins that mediates cell-to-cell adhesion in animal tissues.

calorie A unit of heat. One calorie is the amount of heat needed to raise the temperature of one gram of water by 1°C. Kilocalories (1,000 calories) are used to describe the energy content of foods.

capsid The protein coat of a virus, formed by auto-assembly of one or more proteins into a geometrically symmetrical structure.

carbohydrate A general class of compounds that includes sugars, containing carbon, hydrogen, and oxygen.

carboxyl group A carbon atom attached to an oxygen and a hydroxyl group.

carboxyl terminus The end of a protein containing a carboxyl group.

carcinogen A compound or form of radiation that can cause cancer.

carcinogenesis The formation of a cancer.

carcinoma Cancer of the epithelium, representing the majority of human cancers.

cardiac muscle Muscle of the heart. Composed of myocytes that are linked together in a communication network based on free passage of small molecules through gap junctions.

caspase A protease involved in the initiation of apoptosis.

catabolism Enzyme-regulated breakdown of large molecules for the extraction of chemical-bond energy. Intermediate products are called catabolites.

catalyst A substance that lowers the activation energy of a reaction.

CD28 Cell-surface protein located in T cell membranes, necessary for the activation of T cells by foreign antigens.

cDNA (complementary DNA) DNA that is synthesized from mRNA, thus containing the complementary sequence. cDNA contains coding sequence but not the regulatory sequences that are present in the genome. Labeled probes are made from cDNA for the study of gene expression.

cell adhesion molecule (CAM)   A cell surface protein that is used to connect cells to each other.

cell body   The main part of a cell containing the nucleus, Golgi complex, and endoplasmic reticulum. Used in reference to neurons that have long processes (dendrites and axons) extending some distance from the nucleus and cytoplasmic machinery.

cell coat   See **glycocalyx**.

cell-cycle control system   A team of regulatory proteins that governs progression through the cell cycle.

cell-division-cycle gene (*cdc* gene)   A gene that controls a specific step in the cell cycle.

cell fate   The final differentiated state that a pluripotent embryonic cell is expected to attain.

cell-medicated immune response   Activation of specific cells to launch an immune response against an invading microbe.

cell nuclear replacement   Animal-cloning technique whereby a somatic cell nucleus is transferred to an enucleated oocyte. Synonomous with somatic-cell nuclear transfer.

central nervous system (CNS)   That part of a nervous system that analyzes signals from the body and the environment. In animals, the CNS includes the brain and spinal cord.

centriole   A cylindrical array of microtubules that is found at the center of a centrosome in animal cells.

centromere   A region of a mitotic chromosome that holds sister chromatids together. Microtubules of the spindle fiber connect to an area of the centromere called the kinetochore.

centrosome   Organizes the mitotic spindle and the spindle poles. In most animal cells it contains a pair of centrioles.

chiasma (plural: chiasmata)   An X-shaped connection between homologous chromosomes that occurs during meiosis I, representing a site of crossing-over, or genetic exchange between the two chromosomes.

chromatid   A duplicate chromosome that is still connected to the original at the centromere. The identical pair are called sister chromatids.

chromatin A complex of DNA and proteins (histones and nonhistones) that forms each chromosome and is found in the nucleus of all eukaryotes. Decondensed and threadlike during interphase.

chromatin condensation Compaction of different regions of interphase chromosomes that is mediated by the histones.

chromosome One long molecule of DNA that contains the organism's genes. In prokaryotes, the chromosome is circular and naked; in eukaryotes, it is linear and complexed with histone and nonhistone proteins.

chromosome condensation Compaction of entire chromosomes in preparation for cell division.

clinical breast exam An exam of the breast performed by a physician to check for lumps or other changes.

cyclic adenosine monophosphate (cAMP) A second messenger in a cell-signaling pathway that is produced from ATP by the enzyme adenylate cyclase.

cyclin A protein that activates protein kinases (cyclin-dependent protein kinases, or Cdk) that control progression from one state of the cell cycle to another.

cytochemistry The study of the intracellular distribution of chemicals.

cytochrome Colored, iron-containing protein that is part of the electron transport chain.

cytotoxic T cell A T lymphocyte that kills infected body cells.

dendrite An extension of a nerve cell that receives signals from other neurons.

dexrazoxane A drug used to protect the heart from the toxic effects of anthracycline drugs such as doxorubicin. It belongs to the family of drugs called chemoprotective agents.

dideoxy sequencing A method for sequencing DNA that employs dideoxyribose nucleotides.

diploid A genetic term meaning two sets of homologous chromosomes, one set from the mother and the other from the father. Thus diploid organisms have two versions (alleles) of each gene in the genome.

DNA (deoxyribonucleic acid) A long polymer formed by linking four different kinds of nucleotides together like beads on a string. The sequence of nucleotides is used to encode an organism's genes.

DNA helicase   An enzyme that separates and unwinds the two DNA strands in preparation for replication or transcription.

DNA library   A collection of DNA fragments that are cloned into plasmids or viral genomes.

DNA ligase   An enzyme that joins two DNA strands together to make a continuous DNA molecule.

DNA microarray   A technique for studying the simultaneous expression of a very large number of genes.

DNA polymerase   An enzyme that synthesizes DNA using one strand as a template.

DNA primase   An enzyme that synthesizes a short strand of RNA that serves as a primer for DNA replication.

dorsal   The backside of an animal. Also refers to the upper surface of anatomical structures, such as arms or wings.

dorsoventral   The body axis running from the backside to the frontside or the upperside to the underside of a structure.

double helix   The three-dimensional structure of DNA in which the two strands twist around each other to form a spiral.

doxorubicin   An anticancer drug that belongs to a family of antitumor antibiotics.

Drosophila melanogaster   Small species of fly, commonly called a fruit fly, that is used as an experimental organism in genetics, embryology, and gerontology.

ductal carcinoma in situ (DCIS)   Abnormal cells that involve only the lining of a breast duct. The cells have not spread outside the duct to other tissues in the breast. Also called intraductal carcinoma.

dynein   A motor protein that is involved in chromosome movements during cell division.

dysplasia   Disordered growth of cells in a tissue or organ, often leading to the development of cancer.

ectoderm   An embryonic tissue that is the precursor of the epidermis and the nervous system.

electrochemical gradient   A differential concentration of an ion or molecule across the cell membrane that serves as a source of potential energy and may polarize the cell electrically.

electron microscope   A microscope that uses electrons to produce a high-resolution image of the cell.

embryogensis   The development of an embryo from a fertilized egg.

embryonic stem cell (ES cell)   A pluripotent cell derived from the inner cell mass (the cells that give rise to the embryo instead of the placenta) of a mammalian embryo.

endocrine cell   A cell that is specialized for the production and release of hormones. Such cells make up hormone-producing tissue such as the pituitary gland or gonads.

endocytosis   Cellular uptake of material from the environment by invagination of the cell membrane to form a vesicle called an endosome. The endosome's contents are made available to the cell after it fuses with a lysosome.

endoderm   An embryonic tissue layer that gives rise to the gut.

endoplasmic reticulum (ER)   Membrane-bounded chambers that are used to modify newly synthesized proteins with the addition of sugar molecules (glycosylation). When finished, the glycosylated proteins are sent to the Golgi apparatus in exocytotic vesicles.

endothelial cell   A cell that forms the endothelium, a thin sheet of cells lining the inner surface of all blood vessels.

enhancer   A DNA regulatory sequence that provides a binding site for transcription factors capable of increasing the rate of transcription for a specific gene. Often located thousands of base pairs away from the gene it regulates.

enveloped virus   A virus containing a capsid that is surrounded by a lipid bilayer originally obtained from the membrane of a previously infected cell.

enzyme   A protein or RNA that catalyzes a specific chemical reaction.

epidermis   The epithelial layer, or skin, that covers the outer surface of the body.

ER signal sequence   The amino terminal sequence that directs proteins to enter the endoplasmic reticulum (ER). This sequence is removed once the protein enters the ER.

erythrocyte   A red blood cell that contains the oxygen-carrying pigment hemoglobin used to deliver oxygen to cells in the body.

Escherichia coli (**E. coli**)   Rod shape, gram negative bacterium that inhabits the intestinal tract of most animals and is used as an experimental organism by geneticists and biomedical researchers.

euchromatin Lightly staining portion of interphase chromatin, in contrast to the darkly staining heterochromatin (condensed chromatin). Euchromatin contains most, if not all, of the active genes.

eukaryote (eucaryote) A cell containing a nucleus and many membrane-bounded organelles. All life-forms, except bacteria and viruses, are composed of eukaryote cells.

exocytosis The process by which molecules are secreted from a cell. Molecules to be secreted are located in Golgi-derived vesicles that fuse with the inner surface of the cell membrane, depositing the contents into the intercellular space.

exon Coding region of a eukaryote gene that is represented in messenger RNA, and thus directs the synthesis of a specific protein.

expression studies Examination of the type and quantity of mRNA or protein that is produced by cells, tissues, or organs.

fat A lipid material, consisting of triglycerides (fatty acids bound to glycerol), that is stored in adipocytes as an energy reserve.

fatty acid A compound that has a carboxylic acid attached to a long hydrocarbon chain. A major source of cellular energy and a component of phospholipids.

fertilization The fusion of haploid male and female gametes to form a diploid zygote.

fibroblast The cell type that, by secreting an extracellular matrix, gives rise to the connective tissue of the body.

filter hybridization The detection of specific DNA or RNA molecules, fixed on a nylon filter, by incubating the filter with a labeled probe that hybridizes to the target sequence.

fixative A chemical that is used to preserve cells and tissues. Common examples are formaldehyde, methanol, and acetic acid.

flagellum (plural: flagella) Whiplike structure found in prokaryotes and eukaryotes that are used to propel cells through water.

fluorescein Fluorescent dye that produces a green light when illuminated with ultraviolet or blue light.

fluorescent dye A dye that absorbs UV or blue light and emits light of a longer wavelength, usually as green or red light.

fluorescent microscope A microscope that is equipped with special filters and a beam splitter for the examination of tissues and cells stained with a fluorescent dye.

follicle cell   Cells that surround and help feed a developing oocyte.

G_0   G "zero" refers to a phase of the cell cycle. State of withdrawal from the cycle as the cell enters a resting or quiescent stage. Occurs in differentiated body cells as well as developing oocytes.

G_1   Gap 1 refers to the phase of the cell cycle that occurs just after mitosis and before the next round of DNA synthesis.

G_2   Gap 2 refers to the phase of the cell cycle that follows DNA replication and precedes mitosis.

gap junction   A communication channel in the membranes of adjacent cells that allows free passage of ions and small molecules.

gastrulation   An embryological event in which a spherical embryo is converted into an elongated structure with a head end, a tail end, and a gut (gastrula).

gene   A region of the DNA that specifies a specific protein or RNA molecule that is handed down from one generation to the next. This region includes both the coding, noncoding, and regulatory sequences.

gene regulatory protein   Any protein that binds to DNA and thereby affects the expression of a specific gene.

gene repressor protein   A protein that binds to DNA and blocks transcription of a specific gene.

gene therapy   A method for treating disease whereby a defective gene, causing the disease, is either repaired, replaced, or supplemented with a functional copy.

genetic code   A set of rules that assigns a specific DNA or RNA triplet, consisting of a three-base sequence, to a specific amino acid.

genome   All of the genes that belong to a cell or an organism.

genomic library   A collection of DNA fragments, obtained by digesting genomic DNA with a restriction enzyme, that are cloned into plasmid or viral vectors.

genomics   The study of DNA sequences and their role in the function and structure of an organism.

genotype   The genetic composition of a cell or organism.

germ cell   Cells that develop into gametes, either sperm or oocytes.

glucose   Six-carbon monosaccharide (sugar) that is the principal source of energy for many cells and organisms. Stored as glycogen in animal cells and as starch in plants. Wood is an elaborate polymer of glucose and other sugars.

glycerol A three-carbon alcohol that is an important component of phospholipids.

glycocalyx A molecular "forest," consisting of glycosylated proteins and lipids, that covers the surface of every cell. The glycoproteins and glycolipids, carried to the cell membrane by Golgi-derived vesicles, have many functions, including the formation of ion channels, cell-signaling receptors and transporters.

glycogen A polymer of glucose used to store energy in an animal cell.

glycolysis The degradation of glucose with production of ATP.

glycoprotein Any protein that has a chain of glucose molecules (oligosaccharide) attached to some of the amino acid residues.

glycosylation The process of adding one or more sugar molecules to proteins or lipids.

glycosyl transferase An enzyme in the Golgi complex that adds glucose to proteins.

Golgi complex (Golgi apparatus) Membrane-bounded organelle in eukaryote cells that receives glycoproteins from the ER, which are modified and sorted before being sent to their final destination. The Golgi complex is also the source of glycolipids that are destined for the cell membrane. The glycoproteins and glycolipids leave the Golgi by exocytosis. This organelle is named after the Italian histologist Camillo Golgi, who discovered it in 1898.

granulocyte A type of white blood cell that includes the neutrophils, basophils, and eosinophils.

growth factor A small protein (polypeptide) that can stimulate cells to grow and proliferate.

haploid Having only one set of chromosomes. A condition that is typical in gametes, such as sperm and eggs.

HeLa cell A tumor-derived cell line, originally isolated from a cancer patient in 1951. Currently used by many laboratories to study the cell biology of cancer and carcinogenesis.

helix-loop-helix A structural motif common to a group of gene regulatory proteins.

helper T cell A type of T lymphocyte that helps stimulate B cells to make antibodies directed against a specific microbe or antigen.

hemoglobin An iron-containing protein complex, located in red blood cells that picks up oxygen in the lungs and carries it to other tissues and cells of the body.

hemopoiesis Production of blood cells, occurring primarily in the bone marrow.

hepatocyte A liver cell.

heterochromatin A region of a chromosome that is highly condensed and transcriptionally inactive.

histochemistry The study of chemical differentiation of tissues.

histology The study of tissues.

histone Small nuclear proteins, rich in the amino acids arginine and lysine, that form the nucleosome in eukaryote nuclei, a beadlike structure that is a major component of chromatin.

HIV The human immunodeficiency virus that is responsible for AIDS.

homolog One of two or more genes that have a similar sequence and are descended from a common ancestor gene.

homologous Organs or molecules that are similar in structure because they have descended from a common ancestor. Used primarily in reference to DNA and protein sequences.

homologous chromosomes Two copies of the same chromosome, one inherited from the mother and the other from the father.

hormone A signaling molecule, produced and secreted by endocrine glands. Usually released into general circulation for coordination of an animal's physiology.

housekeeping gene A gene that codes for a protein that is needed by all cells, regardless of the cell's specialization. Genes encoding enzymes involved in glycolysis and the Krebs cycle are common examples.

hybridization A term used in molecular biology (recombinant DNA technology) meaning the formation of a double-stranded nucleic acid through complementary base-pairing. A property that is exploited in filter hybridization, a procedure that is used to screen gene libraries and to study gene structure and expression.

hydrophilic A polar compound that mixes readily with water.

hydrophobic A nonpolar molecule that dissolves in fat and lipid solutions but not in water.

hydroxyl group (-OH)   Chemical group consisting of oxygen and hydrogen that is a prominent part of alcohol.

image analysis   A computerized method for extracting information from digitized microscopic images of cells or cell organelles.

immunofluorescence   Detection of a specific cellular protein with the aid of a fluorescent dye that is coupled to an antibody.

immunoglobulin (Ig)   An antibody made by B cells as part of the adaptive immune response.

incontinence   Inability to control the flow of urine from the bladder (urinary incontinence) or the escape of stool from the rectum (fecal incontinence).

in situ hybridization   A method for studying gene expression, whereby a labeled cDNA or RNA probe hybridizes to a specific mRNA in intact cells or tissues. The procedure is usually carried out on tissue sections or smears of individual cells.

insulin   Polypeptide hormone secreted by β (beta) cells in the vertebrate pancreas. Production of this hormone is regulated directly by the amount of glucose that is in the blood.

interleukin   A small protein hormone, secreted by lymphocytes, to activate and coordinate the adaptive immune response.

interphase   The period between each cell division, which includes the G_1, S, and G_2 phases of the cell cycle.

intron   A section of a eukaryotic gene that is noncoding. It is transcribed, but does not appear in the mature mRNA.

in vitro   Refers to cells growing in culture, or a biochemical reaction occurring in a test tube (Latin for "in glass").

in vivo   A biochemical reaction, or a process, occurring in living cells or a living organism (Latin for "in life").

ion   An atom that has gained or lost electrons, thus acquiring a charge. Common examples are Na^+ and Ca^{++} ions.

ion channel   A transmembrane channel that allows ions to diffuse across the membrane and down their electrochemical gradient.

Jak-STAT signaling pathway   One of several cell-signaling pathways that activates gene expression. The pathway is activated through cell-surface receptors and cytoplasmic Janus kinases (Jaks), and signal transducers and activators of transcription (STATs).

karyotype   A pictorial catalog of a cell's chromosomes, showing their number, size, shape, and overall banding pattern.

keratin   Proteins produced by specialized epithelial cells called keratinocytes. Keratin is found in hair, fingernails, and feathers.

kinesin   A motor protein that uses energy obtained from the hydrolysis of ATP to move along a microtubule.

kinetochore   A complex of proteins that forms around the centromere of mitotic or meiotic chromosomes, providing an attachment site for microtubules. The other end of each microtubule is attached to a chromosome.

Krebs cycle (citric acid cycle)   The central metabolic pathway in all eukaryotes and aerobic prokaryotes, discovered by the German chemist Hans Krebs in 1937. The cycle oxidizes acetyl groups derived from food molecules. The end products are CO_2, H_2O, and high-energy electrons, which pass via NADH and FADH2 to the respiratory chain. In eukaryotes, the Krebs cycle is located in the mitochondria.

labeling reaction   The addition of a radioactive atom or fluorescent dye to DNA or RNA for use as a probe in filter hybridization.

lagging strand   One of the two newly synthesized DNA strands at a replication fork. The lagging strand is synthesized discontinuously, and therefore, its completion lags behind the second, or leading, strand.

lambda bacteriophage   A viral parasite that infects bacteria. Widely used as a DNA cloning vector.

leading strand   One of the two newly synthesized DNA strands at a replication fork. The leading strand is made by continuous synthesis in the 5' to 3' direction.

leucine zipper   A structural motif of DNA binding proteins, in which two identical proteins are joined together at regularly spaced leucine residues, much like a zipper, to form a dimer.

leukemia   Cancer of white blood cells.

lipid bilayer   Two closely aligned sheets of phospholipids that form the core structure of all cell membranes. The two layers are aligned such that the hydrophobic tails are interior, while the hydrophilic head groups are exterior on both surfaces.

liposome   An artificial lipid bilayer vesicle used in membrane studies and as an artificial gene therapy vector.

locus   A term from genetics that refers to the position of a gene along a chromosome. Different alleles of the same gene occupy the same locus.

long-term potentiation (LTP)   A physical remodeling of synaptic junctions that receive continuous stimulation.

lymphocyte   A type of white blood cell that is involved in the adaptive immune response. There are two kinds of lymphocytes: T lymphocytes and B lymphocytes. T lymphocytes (T cells) mature in the thymus and attack invading microbes directly. B lymphocytes (B cells) mature in the bone marrow and make antibodies that are designed to immobilize or destroy specific microbes or antigens.

lysis   The rupture of the cell membrane followed by death of the cell.

lysosome   Membrane-bounded organelle of eukaryotes that contains powerful digestive enzymes.

macromolecule   A very large molecule that is built from smaller molecular subunits. Common examples are DNA, proteins, and polysaccharides.

magnetic resonance imaging (MRI)   A procedure in which radio waves and a powerful magnet linked to a computer are used to create detailed pictures of areas inside the body. These pictures can show the difference between normal and diseased tissue. MRI makes better images of organs and soft tissue than other scanning techniques, such as CT or X-ray. MRI is especially useful for imaging the brain, spine, the soft tissue of joints, and the inside of bones. Also called nuclear magnetic resonance imaging.

major histocompatibility complex   Vertebrate genes that code for a large family of cell-surface glycoproteins that bind foreign antigens and present them to T cells to induce an immune response.

malignant   Refers to the functional status of a cancer cell that grows aggressively and is able to metastasize, or colonize, other areas of the body.

mammography   The use of X-rays to create a picture of the breast.

MAP-kinase (mitogen-activated protein kinase)   A protein kinase that is part of a cell proliferation–inducing signaling pathway.

M-cyclin   A eukaryote enzyme that regulates mitosis.

meiosis A special form of cell division by which haploid gametes are produced. This is accomplished with two rounds of cell division but only one round of DNA replication.

melanocyte A skin cell that produces the pigment melanin.

membrane The lipid bilayer, and the associated glycocalyx, that surrounds and encloses all cells.

membrane channel A protein complex that forms a pore or channel through the membrane for the free passage of ions and small molecules.

membrane potential A buildup of charged ions on one side of the cell membrane establishes an electrochemical gradient that is measured in millivolts (mV). An important characteristic of neurons as it provides the electric current, when ion channels open, that enable these cells to communicate with each other.

mesoderm An embryonic germ layer that gives rise to muscle, connective tissue, bones, and many internal organs.

messenger RNA (mRNA) An RNA transcribed from a gene that is used as the gene template by the ribosomes, and other components of the translation machinery, to synthesize a protein.

metabolism The sum total of the chemical processes that occur in living cells.

metaphase The stage of mitosis at which the chromosomes are attached to the spindle but have not begun to move apart.

metaphase plate Refers to the imaginary plane established by the chromosomes as they line up at right angles to the spindle poles.

metaplasia A change in the pattern of cellular behavior that often precedes the development of cancer.

metastasis Spread of cancer cells from the site of the original tumor to other parts of the body.

methyl group (-CH$_3$) Hydrophobic chemical group derived from methane. Occurs at the end of a fatty acid.

micrograph Photograph taken through a light, or electron, microscope.

micrometer (μm or micron) Equal to 10^{-6} meters.

microtubule A fine cylindrical tube made of the protein tubulin, forming a major component of the eukaryote cytoskeleton.

millimeter (mm) Equal to 10^{-3} meters.

mitochondrion (plural: mitochondria)   Eukaryote organelle, formerly free-living, that produces most of the cell's ATP.

mitogen   A hormone or signaling molecule that stimulates cells to grow and divide.

mitosis   Division of a eukaryotic nucleus. From the Greek *mitos,* meaning "a thread," in reference to the threadlike appearance of interphase chromosomes.

mitotic chromosome   Highly condensed duplicated chromosomes held together by the centromere. Each member of the pair is referred to as a sister chromatid.

mitotic spindle   Array of microtubules, fanning out from the polar centrioles and connecting to each of the chromosomes.

molecule   Two or more atoms linked together by covalent bonds.

monoclonal antibody   An antibody produced from a B cell–derived clonal line. Since all of the cells are clones of the original B cell, the antibodies produced are identical.

monocyte   A type of white blood cell that is involved in the immune response.

motif   An element of structure or pattern that may be a recurring domain in a variety of proteins.

M phase   The period of the cell cycle (mitosis or meiosis) when the chromosomes separate and migrate to the opposite poles of the spindle.

multipass transmembrane protein   A membrane protein that passes back and forth across the lipid bilayer.

mutant   A genetic variation within a population.

mutation   A heritable change in the nucleotide sequence of a chromosome.

myelin sheath   Insulation applied to the axons of neurons. The sheath is produced by oligodendrocytes in the central nervous system and by Schwann cells in the peripheral nervous system.

myeloid cell   White blood cells other than lymphocytes.

myoblast   Muscle precursor cell. Many myoblasts fuse into a syncytium, containing many nuclei, to form a single muscle cell.

myocyte   A muscle cell.

NAD (nicotine adenine dinucleotide)   Accepts a hydride ion (H^-), produced by the Krebs cycle, forming NADH, the main carrier of electrons for oxidative phosphorylation.

NADH dehydrogenase Removes electrons from NADH and passes them down the electron transport chain.

nanometer (nm) Equal to 10^{-9} meters or 10^{-3} microns.

natural killer cell (NK cell) A lymphocyte that kills virus-infected cells in the body. It also kills foreign cells associated with a tissue or organ transplant.

neuromuscular junction A special form of synapse between a motor neuron and a skeletal muscle cell.

neuron A cell specially adapted for communication that forms the nervous system of all animals.

neurotransmitter A chemical released by neurons at a synapse that transmits a signal to another neuron.

non-small-cell lung cancer A group of lung cancers that includes squamous cell carcinoma, adenocarcinoma, and large cell carcinoma. The small cells are endocrine cells.

northern blotting A technique for the study of gene expression. Messenger RNA (mRNA) is fractionated on an agarose gel and then transferred to a piece of nylon filter paper (or membrane). A specific mRNA is detected by hybridization with a labeled DNA or RNA probe. The original blotting technique invented by E. M. Southern inspired the name.

nuclear envelope The double membrane (two lipid bilayers) enclosing the cell nucleus.

nuclear localization signal (NLS) A short amino acid sequence located on proteins that are destined for the cell nucleus after they are translated in the cytoplasm.

nucleic acid DNA or RNA, a macromolecule consisting of a chain of nucleotides.

nucleolar organizer Region of a chromosome containing a cluster of ribosomal RNA genes that gives rise to the nucleolus.

nucleolus A structure in the nucleus where ribosomal RNA is transcribed and ribosomal subunits are assembled.

nucleoside A purine or pyrimidine linked to a ribose or deoxyribose sugar.

nucleosome A beadlike structure, consisting of histone proteins.

nucleotide A nucleoside containing one or more phosphate groups linked to the 5' carbon of the ribose sugar. DNA and RNA are nucleotide polymers.

nucleus   Eukaryote cell organelle that contains the DNA genome on one or more chromosomes.

oligodendrocyte   A myelinating glia cell of the vertebrate central nervous system.

oligo labeling   A method for incorporating labeled nucleotides into a short piece of DNA or RNA. Also known as the random-primer labeling method.

oligomer   A short polymer, usually consisting of amino acids (oligopeptides), sugars (oligosaccharides), or nucleotides (oligonucleotides). Taken from the Greek word *oligos,* meaning "few" or "little."

oncogene   A mutant form of a normal cellular gene, known as a proto-oncogene, that can transform a cell to a cancerous phenotype.

oocyte   A female gamete or egg cell.

operator   A region of a prokaryote chromosome that controls the expression of adjacent genes.

operon   Two or more prokaryote genes that are transcribed into a single mRNA.

organelle   A membrane-bounded structure, occurring in eukaryote cells, that has a specialized function. Examples are the nucleus, Golgi complex, and endoplasmic reticulum.

osmosis   The movement of solvent across a semipermeable membrane that separates a solution with a high concentration of solutes from one with a low concentration of solutes. The membrane must be permeable to the solvent but not to the solutes. In the context of cellular osmosis, the solvent is always water, the solutes are ions and molecules, and the membrane is the cell membrane.

osteoblast   Cells that form bones.

ovulation   Rupture of a mature follicle with subsequent release of a mature oocyte from the ovary.

oxidative phosphorylation   Generation of high-energy electrons from food molecules that are used to power the synthesis of ATP from ADP and inorganic phosphate. The electrons are eventually transferred to oxygen to complete the process. Occurs in bacteria and mitochondria.

p53   A tumor-suppressor gene that is mutated in about half of all human cancers. The normal function of the *p53* protein is to block passage through the cell cycle when DNA damage is detected.

parthenogenesis   A natural form of animal cloning whereby an individual is produced without the formation of haploid gametes and the fertilization of an egg.

pathogen   An organism that causes disease.

PCR (polymerase chain reaction)   A method for amplifying specific regions of DNA by temperature cycling a reaction mixture containing the template, a heat-stable DNA polymerase, and replication primers.

peptide bond   The chemical bond that links amino acids together to form a protein.

pH   Measures the acidity of a solution as a negative logarithmic function (p) of H^+ concentration (H). Thus a pH of 2.0 (10^{-2} molar H^+) is acidic, whereas a pH of 8.0 (10^{-8} molar H^+) is basic.

phagocyte   A cell that engulfs other cells or debris by phagocytosis.

phagocytosis   A process whereby cells engulf other cells or organic material by endocytosis. A common practice among protozoans and cells of the vertebrate immune system. (Derived from the Greek word *phagein,* "to eat.")

phenotype   Physical characteristics of a cell or organism.

phospholipid   The kind of lipid molecule used to construct cell membranes. Composed of a hydrophilic head-group, phosphate, glycerol, and two hydrophobic fatty acid tails.

phosphorylation   A chemical reaction in which a phosphate is covalently bonded to another molecule.

photoreceptor   A molecule or cell that responds to light.

photosynthesis   A biochemical process in which plants, algae, and certain bacteria use energy obtained from sunlight to synthesize macromolecules from CO_2 and H_2O.

phylogeny   The evolutionary history of an organism, or group of organisms, often represented diagrammatically as a phylogenetic tree.

pinocytosis   A form of endocytosis whereby fluid is brought into the cell from the environment.

placebo   An inactive substance that looks the same, and is administered in the same way, as a drug in a clinical trial.

plasmid   A minichromosome, often carrying antibiotic-resistant genes, that occurs naturally among prokaryotes. Used extensively as a DNA cloning vector.

platelet   A cell fragment, derived from megakaryocytes and lacking a nucleus, that is present in the bloodstream and is involved in blood coagulation.

ploidy   The total number of chromosomes (n) that a cell has. Ploidy is also measured as the amount of DNA (C) in a given cell relative to a haploid nucleus of the same organism. Most organisms are diploid, having two sets of chromosomes, one from each parent, but there is great variation among plants and animals. The silk gland of the moth *Bombyx mori,* for example, has cells that are extremely polyploid, reaching values of 100,000C. Flowers are often highly polyploid, and vertebrate hepatocytes may be 16C.

point mutation   A change in DNA, particularly in a region containing a gene, that alters a single nucleotide.

polyploid   Possessing more than two sets of homologous chromosomes.

portal system   A system of liver vessels that carries liver enzymes directly to the digestive tract.

probe   Usually a fragment of a cloned DNA molecule that is labeled with a radioisotope or fluorescent dye and used to detect specific DNA or RNA molecules on Southern or northern blots.

promoter   A DNA sequence to which RNA polymerase binds to initiate gene transcription.

prophase   The first stage of mitosis. The chromosomes are duplicated and beginning to condense but are attached to the spindle.

protein   A major constituent of cells and organisms. Proteins, made by linking amino acids together, are used for structural purposes and regulate many biochemical reactions in their alternative role as enzymes. Proteins range in size from just a few amino acids to more than 200.

protein glycosylation   The addition of sugar molecules to a protein.

proto-oncogene   A normal gene that can be converted to a cancer-causing gene (oncogene) by a point mutation or through inappropriate expression.

protozoa   Free-living, single-cell eukaryotes that feed on bacteria and other microorganisms. Common examples are *Paramecium* and *Amoeba*. Parasitic forms are also known that inhabit the digestive and urogenital tract of many animals, including humans.

purine   A nitrogen-containing compound that is found in RNA and DNA. Two examples are adenine and guanine.

pyrimidine   A nitrogen-containing compound found in RNA and DNA. Examples are cytosine, thymine, and uracil (RNA only).

radioactive isotope   An atom with an unstable nucleus that emits radiation as it decays.

randomized clinical trial   A study in which the participants are assigned by chance to separate groups that compare different treatments; neither the researchers nor the participants can choose which group. Using chance to assign people to groups means that the groups will be similar and that the treatments they receive can be compared objectively. At the time of the trial, it is not known which treatment is best.

reagent   A chemical solution designed for a specific biochemical or histochemical procedure.

recombinant DNA   A DNA molecule that has been formed by joining two or more fragments from different sources.

regulatory sequence   A DNA sequence to which proteins bind that regulate the assembly of the transcriptional machinery.

replication bubble   Local dissociation of the DNA double helix in preparation for replication. Each bubble contains two replication forks.

replication fork   The Y-shaped region of a replicating chromosome. Associated with replication bubbles.

replication origin (origin of replication, ORI)   The location at which DNA replication begins.

respiratory chain (electron transport chain)   A collection of iron- and copper-containing proteins, located in the inner mitochondrion membrane, that utilize the energy of electrons traveling down the chain to synthesize ATP.

restriction enzyme   An enzyme that cuts DNA at specific sites.

restriction map   The size and number of DNA fragments obtained after digesting with one or more restriction enzymes.

retrovirus   A virus that converts its RNA genome to DNA once it has infected a cell.

reverse transcriptase   An RNA-dependent DNA polymerase. This enzyme synthesizes DNA by using RNA as a template, the reverse of the usual flow of genetic information from DNA to RNA.

ribosomal RNA (rRNA) RNA that is part of the ribosome and serves both a structural and functional role, possibly by catalyzing some of the steps involved in protein synthesis.

ribosome A complex of protein and RNA that catalyzes the synthesis of proteins.

rough endoplasmic reticulum (rough ER) Endoplasmic reticulum that has ribosomes bound to its outer surface.

Saccharomyces Genus of budding yeast that are frequently used in the study of eukaryote cell biology.

sarcoma Cancer of connective tissue.

Schwann cell Glia cell that produces myelin in the peripheral nervous system.

screening Checking for disease when there are no symptoms.

senescence Physical and biochemical changes that occur in cells and organisms with age.

signal transduction A process by which a signal is relayed to the interior of a cell where it elicits a response at the cytoplasmic or nuclear level.

smooth muscle cell Muscles lining the intestinal tract and arteries. Lacks the striations typical of cardiac and skeletal muscle, giving it a smooth appearance when viewed under a microscope.

somatic cell Any cell in a plant or animal except those that produce gametes (germ cells or germ cell precursors).

somatic cell nuclear transfer Animal cloning technique whereby a somatic cell nucleus is transferred to an enucleated oocyte. Synonomous with cell nuclear replacement.

Southern blotting The transfer of DNA fragments from an agarose gel to a piece of nylon filter paper. Specific fragments are identified by hybridizing the filter to a labeled probe. Invented by the Scottish scientist E. M. Southern in 1975.

stem cell Pluripotent progenitor cell, found in embryos and various parts of the body, that can differentiate into a wide variety of cell types.

steroid A hydrophobic molecule with a characteristic four-ringed structure. Sex hormones, such as estrogen and testosterone, are steroids.

structural gene A gene that codes for a protein or an RNA. Distinguished from regions of the DNA that are involved in regulating gene expression but are noncoding.

synapse A neural communication junction between an axon and a dendrite. Signal transmission occurs when neurotransmitters, released into the junction by the axon of one neuron, stimulate receptors on the dendrite of a second neuron.

syncytium A large multinucleated cell. Skeletal muscle cells are syncytiums produced by the fusion of many myoblasts.

syngeneic transplants A patient receives tissue or an organ from an identical twin.

tamoxifen A drug that is used to treat breast cancer. Tamoxifen blocks the effects of the hormone estrogen in the body. It belongs to the family of drugs called antiestrogens.

T cell (T lymphocyte) A white blood cell involved in activating and coordinating the immune response.

telomere The end of a chromosome. Replaced by the enzyme telomerase with each round of cell division to prevent shortening of the chromosomes.

telophase The final stage of mitosis in which the chromosomes decondense and the nuclear envelope reforms.

template A single strand of DNA or RNA whose sequence serves as a guide for the synthesis of a complementary, or daughter, strand.

therapeutic cloning The cloning of a human embryo for the purpose of harvesting the inner cell mass (ES cells).

topoisomerase An enzyme that makes reversible cuts in DNA to relieve strain or to undo knots.

transcription The copying of a DNA sequence into RNA, catalyzed by RNA polymerase.

transcriptional factor A general term referring to a wide assortment of proteins needed to initiate or regulate transcription.

transfection Introduction of a foreign gene into a eukaryote cell.

transfer RNA (tRNA) A collection of small RNA molecules that transfer an amino acid to a growing polypeptide chain on a ribosome. There is a separate tRNA for amino acid.

transgenic organism A plant or animal that has been transfected with a foreign gene.

trans-Golgi network The membrane surfaces where glycoproteins and glycolipids exit the Golgi complex in transport vesicles.

translation A ribosome-catalyzed process whereby the nucleotide sequence of an mRNA is used as a template to direct the synthesis of a protein.

transposable element (transposon) A segment of DNA that can move from one region of a genome to another.

ultrasound (ultrasonography) A procedure in which high-energy sound waves (ultrasound) are bounced off internal tissues or organs producing echoes that are used to form a picture of body tissues (a sonogram).

umbilical cord blood stem cells Stem cells, produced by a human fetus and the placenta, that are found in the blood that passes from the placenta to the fetus.

vector A virus or plasmid used to carry a DNA fragment into a bacterial cell (for cloning) or into a eukaryote to produce a transgenic organism.

vesicle A membrane-bounded bubble found in eukaryote cells. Vesicles carry material from the ER to the Golgi and from the Golgi to the cell membrane.

virus A particle containing an RNA or DNA genome surrounded by a protein coat. Viruses are cellular parasites that cause many diseases.

western blotting The transfer of protein from a polyacrylamide gel to a piece of nylon filter paper. Specific proteins are detected with labeled antibodies. The name was inspired by the original blotting technique invented by E. M. Southern.

yeast Common term for unicellular eukaryotes that are used to brew beer and make bread. Bakers yeast, *Saccharomyces cerevisiae,* is also widely used in studies on cell biology.

zygote A diploid cell produced by the fusion of a sperm and egg.

FURTHER READING

ᗌᗍ

Alberts, Bruce. *Essential Cell Biology.* New York: Garland Publishing, 1998.

Aldwin, Carolyn, and Diane Gilmer. *Health, Illness and Optimal Aging: Biological and Psychosocial Perspectives.* London: Sage Publications, 2003.

American Institute for Cancer Research. "Diets High in Fiber Cut Risk of Colon Cancer Nearly in Half." Press Release, May 2, 2003. Available online. URL: http://www.aicr.org/presscorner/pubsearchdetail.lasso?index=1619. Accessed on March 5, 2004.

American Institute for Cancer Research. "New Scientific Thinking Implicates Body Fat as Cancer Promoter." Press Release, July 11, 2002. Available online. URL: http://www.aicr.org/press/pressrelease.lasso?index=1473. Accessed on March 5, 2004.

American Institute of Physics. "Madam Curie." Available online. URL: http://www.aip.org/history/curie/radinst3.htm. Accessed on March 5, 2004.

Beers, Mark H., and Robert Berkow, editors. *The Merck Manual of Geriatrics.* New Jersey: Merck Research Laboratories, 2000.

Dr. Bob's All Creature Site. "The Life Span of Animals." This site is maintained by a veterinary hospital in California. Available online. URL: http://www.sonic.net/~petdoc/lifespan.htm. Accessed on March 5, 2004.

Fish BC, British Columbia, Canada. "The White Surgeon." Available online. URL: http://www.bcadventure.com/adventure/angling/game_fish/sturgeon.phtml. Accessed on March 5, 2004.

Hayflick, Leonard. "How and Why We Age." *Exp Gerontol* Vol. 33 (1998): 639–653.

Human Genome Program of the U.S. Department of Energy. "Gene Therapy." Available online. URL: http://www.ornl.gov/TechResources/Human_Genome/medicine/genetherapy.html. Accessed on March 5, 2004.

Humber, James M., and Robert F. Almeder. *Care of the Aged.* New Jersey: Humana Press, 2003.

Institute of Medicine, Washington, DC. "Improving the Quality of Long Term Care." Available online. URL: http://www.iom.edu/file. asp?id=4136. Accessed on March 5, 2004.

Institute of Molecular Biotechnology. Jena, Germany. "Molecules of life." Available online. URL: http://www.imb-jena.de/IMAGE.html. Accessed on February 20, 2004.

Kane, Robert L., Joseph G. Ouslander, and Itamar B. Abrass. *Essentials of Clinical Geriatrics.* New York: McGraw-Hill, 2003.

Krstic, R. V. *Illustrated Encyclopedia of Human Histology.* New York: Springer-Verlag, 1984.

Lentz, Thomas L. *Cell Fine Structure: An Atlas of Drawings of Whole-Cell Structure.* Philadelphia: Saunders, 1971.

Lovell-Badge, R. "The Future of Stem Cell Research." *Nature* Vol. 414 (2001): 88–91.

Mader, Sylvia S. *Inquiry into Life.* Boston: McGraw-Hill, 2003.

Magalhães, João Pedro de, and Olivier Toussaint. "The Evolution of Mammalian Aging." *Experimental Gerontology* Volume 37 (2002): 769–775.

National Center for Biotechnology Information. "Genes and Disease." Chromosome maps of all genes known to cause human diseases. Available online. URL: http://www.ncbi.nlm.nih.gov:80/books/bv. fcgi?call=bv.View.ShowTOC&rid=gnd.TOC&depth=2. Accessed on March 5, 2004.

National Institute of Arthritis and Musculoskeletal and Skin Disease. "Handout on Health: Osteoarthritis." Available online. URL: http://www.niams.nih.gov/hi/topics/arthritis/oahandout.htm. Accessed on March 5, 2004.

National Institute of Arthritis and Musculoskeletal and Skin Disease. "Handout on Health: Rheumatoid Arthritis." Available online. URL: http://www.niams.nih.gov/hi/topics/arthritis/rahandout.html. Accessed on March 5, 2004.

National Institute of Arthritis and Musculoskeletal and Skin Disease. "Osteoporosis: Progress and Promise." Available online. URL:

http://www.niams.nih.gov/hi/topics/osteoporosis/opbkgr.htm. Accessed on March 5, 2004.

National Institutes of Health. "Age and Preexisting Health Problems Affect the Prognosis and Treatment Options of Older Breast Cancer Patients." News release, February 20, 2001. Available online. URL: http://www.nia.nih.gov/news/pr/2001/0220.htm. Accessed on October 25, 2003.

National Institutes of Health. "Findings Show Exceptional Longevity Runs in Families." Available online. URL: http://www.nia.nih.gov/news/pr/2002/0610.htm. Accessed on March 5, 2004.

National Institutes of Health. "Folic Acid Possibly a Key Factor in Alzheimer's Disease Prevention." Available online. URL: http://www.nih.gov/news/pr/mar2002/nia-01.htm. Accessed on March 5, 2004.

National Institutes of Health. "Stem Cell Information." Available online. URL: http://stemcells.nih.gov/index.asp. Accessed on March 5, 2004.

Nature. "Double Helix:50 Years of DNA." Many articles assembled by the journal to commemorate the 50th anniversary of James Watson and Francis Crick's classic paper describing the structure of DNA. Available online. URL: http://www.nature.com/nature/dna50/index.html. Accessed on March 5, 2004.

Nature Science Update. "Alzheimer's Vaccine Setback Confirmed." March 17, 2003. Available online. URL: http://www.nature.com/nsu/030310/030310-15.html. Accessed on March 5, 2004.

Nature Science Update. "Hope for Alzheimer's Vaccine." May 22, 2003. Available online. URL: http://www.nature.com/nsu/030519/030519-7.html. Accessed on March 5, 2004.

Nature Science Update. "Supplement Brakes Parkinson's: Coenzyme Q10 May Delay Brain Degeneration." October 15, 2002. Available online. URL: http://www.nature.com/nsu/021014/021014-3.html. Accessed on March 5, 2004.

Nature-Wildlife.com. "The Elephant, *Loxodonta africana.*" Available online. URL: http://nature-wildlife.com/eletxt.htm. Accessed on March 5, 2004.

The New York Times. "As More Live Past a Century, 100 Isn't What It Used to Be." January 20, 2003. Available online. URL: http://www.nytimes.com/2003/01/20/nyregion/20CENT.html. Accessed on March 5, 2004.

The New York Times. "At Age 4,600-Plus, Methuselah Pine Tree Begets New Offspring." June 17, 2003. Available online. URL: http://www.nytimes.com/2003/06/17/science/17TREE.html. Accessed on March 5, 2004.

The New York Times. "Bone Marrow Found to Have Cells to Repair the Pancreas." March 15, 2003. Available online. URL: http://www.nytimes.com/2003/03/15/health/15STEM.html. Accessed on March 5, 2004.

The New York Times. "Hormone Replacement Study a Shock to the Medical System." July 10, 2002. Available online. URL: http://www.nytimes.com/2002/07/10/health/10HORM.html. Accessed on March 5, 2004.

The New York Times. "Hormone Use Found to Raise Dementia Risk." May 28, 2003. Available online. URL: http://www.nytimes.com/2003/05/28/health/28HORM.html. Accessed on March 5, 2004.

The New York Times. "Low-Calorie-Diet Study Takes Scientists Aback." September 19, 2003. Available online. URL: http://www.nytimes.com/2003/09/19/science/19DIET.html. Accessed on March 5, 2004.

The New York Times. "Male Hormone Therapy Popular but Untested." August 19, 2002. Available online. URL: http://www.nytimes.com/ 2002/08/19/health/19HORM.html. Accessed on October 25, 2003.

The New York Times. "New Ideas Energize Alzheimer's Battle." January 14, 2003. Available online. URL: http://www.nytimes.com/2003/01/14/health/14DEME.html. Accessed on March 5, 2004.

The New York Times. "Politically Correct Stem Cell Is Licensed to Biotech Concern." December 11, 2002. Available online. URL: http://www.nytimes.com/2002/12/11/business/11STEM.html. Accessed on March 5, 2004.

The New York Times. "Study Recommends Not Using Hormone Therapy for Bone Loss." October 1, 2003. Available online. URL: http://www.nytimes.com/2003/10/01/health/01HORM.html. Accessed on March 5, 2004.

Olshansky, S. J., Leonard Hayflick, and B. A. Carnes. "Position Statement on Human Aging." *J Gerontol* 57A (2002): B292–B297.

Scientific American. "Cell Communication: The Inside Story." June 20, 2000. Available online. URL: http://www.sciam.com/print_version.

cfm?articleID=0001998E-5F5A-1C74-9B81809EC588EF21. Accessed
on March 5, 2004.
Whitbourne, Susan Krauss. *The Aging Individual: Physical and Psychological Perspectives.* New York: Springer Publishing Company, 2002.

WEB SITES

The Department of Energy Human Genome Project (United States).
Covers every aspect of the human genome project including appli-
cations to gene therapy. http://www.ornl.gov/TechResources/
Human_Genome. Accessed on October 25, 2003.

Gene Therapy Department, University of Southern California.
http://www.humangenetherapy.com. Accessed on October 25,
2003.

**Genetic Science Learning Center at the Eccles Institute of Human
Genetics, University of Utah.** An excellent resource for beginning
students. This site contains information and illustrations covering
basic cell biology, animal cloning, gene therapy, and stem cells.
http://gslc.genetics.utah.edu. Accessed on October 25, 2003.

Institute of Molecular Biotechnology, Jena/Germany. Image Library
of Biological Macromolecules. http://www.imb-jena.de/IMAGE.
html. Accessed on October 25, 2003.

National Center for Biotechnology Information (NCBI). This site,
established by the National Institutes of Health, is an excellent
resource for anyone interested in biology. The NCBI provides
access to GenBank (DNA sequences), literature databases (Medline and others), molecular databases, and topics dealing with
genomic biology. With the literature database, for example, anyone
can access Medline's 11 million biomedical journal citations to
research biomedical questions. Many of these links provide free
access to full-length research papers. http://www.ncbi.nlm.nih.gov.
Accessed on October 25, 2003.

The National Human Genome Research Institute (United States).
The institute supports genetic and genomic research, including the
ethical, legal, and social implications of genetics research.
http://www.genome.gov. Accessed on October 25, 2003.

National Institutes of Health (United States). Links to gerontology and geriatrics articles. http://www.ncbi.nlm.nih.gov. Accessed on October 25, 2003.

National Institute on Aging. http://www.nia.nih.gov. Accessed on October 25, 2003.

Nature. The journal *Nature* has provided a comprehensive guide to the human genome. This site provides links to the definitive historical record for the sequences and analyses of human chromosomes. All papers, which can be downloaded for free, are based on the final draft produced by the Human Genome Project. http://www. nature.com/nature/focus/humangenome/. Accessed on October 25, 2003.

The World Health Organization. Extensive coverage of age-related issues throughout the world. http://www.who.int/en. Accessed on October 25, 2003.

INDEX